Betrayal and Forgiveness

How to Navigate the Turmoil and Learn to Trust Again

Dr. Bruce Chalmer

Also by Dr. Bruce Chalmer

Understanding Statistics (1986)

Reigniting the Spark: Why Stable Relationships Lose Intimacy, and How to Get It Back (2020)

It's Not About Communication! Why Everything You Know About Couples Therapy is Wrong (2022)

Published by Someware Publishing

Cover design by Annemarie Lamprecht

ISBN Paperback: 979-8-9907504-0-1
ISBN eBook: 979-8-9907504-1-8

Praise for *Betrayal and Forgiveness*

Dr. Chalmer offers clear, compassionate guidance on how to heal from betrayal—with or without forgiving the offender or restoring your relationship. **I recommend this book to both hurt parties and those who want to help them heal. –Janis Abrahms Spring, Ph.D.**, author of *After the Affair* and *How Can I Forgive You? The Courage to Forgive, The Freedom Not To*

What a wonderful book! If you have ever felt betrayed in a relationship, *Betrayal and Forgiveness* is an important roadmap to being able to trust and love again. Through stories of betrayal in real-life people and couples, **you will feel seen and understood.** Then you will be taken on a journey of understanding, faith, and practical advice to find the most loving way forward. I loved Dr. Chalmer's exploration of faith as part of the healing process. And I was dying to find out what happened to the couples. I'm so glad he told us! – **Katrina Bos**, author of *Tantric Intimacy: Discover the Magic of True Connection*

A guiding light for the betrayed, Dr. Bruce Chalmer's wise and compassionate book escorts you on a courageous journey toward understanding and forgiving others and yourself, after even the most devastating upheavals. –**MB Caschetta**, author of *A Cheerleader's Guide to Spiritual Enlightenment*

Whether you're a client or a clinician, Dr. Bruce Chalmer's latest book *Betrayal and Forgiveness* offers spectacular insight into the rich landscape of couples therapy. **I highly recommend Betrayal and Forgiveness for clinicians and clients alike. –Jane Kast, M.A.,** psychologist

Bravo! *Betrayal and Forgiveness* **is a clear, easy to read, and relatable book for anyone struggling with these topics.** It gives clear guidance to those who have been stung by betrayal, those who have betrayed, and the therapists and coaches who work with them. I highly recommend this book to anyone seeking to understand how to navigate the aftermath of betrayal and for those who yearn to heal.—**Karin Calde, Ph.D., CPC**, Relationship and Self-Development Coach and host of podcast, "Love is Us"

"Forgiveness is an inside job" is a powerful and necessary concept Dr. Chalmer motivates the reader to embrace. –**Dr. Deborah S. Miller**, author of *More Than Sorry: 5 Steps to Deepen Your Apology After You Have Committed Infidelity*

Praise for *It's Not About Communication*

Dr. Bruce Chalmer's book *It's Not About Communication* takes the reader "behind the curtain" of the whole couples therapy process. He demystifies the often mysterious and unknown experience of therapy so that couples know what to expect as soon as they walk through the door. Compassionate and informative, along with using a bit of humor, Dr. Chalmer shares his wealth of knowledge that comes from years of treating couples. **I recommend this book to both therapists and couples alike** who are looking for a roadmap of the couples therapy process. –**Dr. Alyson Nerenberg**, author of *No Perfect Love- Shattering the Illusion of Flawless Relationships*

If you're stuck in your relationship this book may be the catalyst you need to have the relationship you want. — **Susan Bratton**, "Intimacy Expert to Millions"

Unlike so much of the help on offer these days, Dr. Chalmer offers an engagingly and endearingly clear path to this way to feel at home in the universe. **A breakthrough book for couples ready at long last to brave reality in all of its paradoxical splendor.** –**Jeremy Sherman**, author of *What's Up With A**holes? A Beginner's Guide to Advanced Psychoproctology*

Written in an accessible, conversational style, this book provides the unexpected solution to relationship problems in couples. Based on three key ideas and illustrated with case examples from clinical practice, Dr. Chalmer highlights the steps to lasting change. **A worthy** resource for both couples and therapists who want to be effective. –**Dr. Paul Foxman**, author of *Dancing With Fear*

Praise for *Reigniting the Spark*

Reading this book is like breathing fresh Vermont air— refreshing, inspiring, down-to-earth, and filled with grounded wisdom that emerges from decades of practice as a therapist with hundreds of couples... I am especially inspired by his willingness to bring spiritual lives--religious and nonreligious-into the conversation, exploring with couples what matters most to each of them, while dealing with life's inevitable uncertainties and struggles. –**Peggy Sax**, psychologist and Executive Director of Reauthoring Teaching

This book is concise, but it is **so well written that it feels like we are sitting in his office or laying on his couch, talking about what we want and asking how we can get there.** He shows us how to lay a foundation for intimacy and trust that will connect us to our partner for years to come. He also makes us take a look at all the reasons we should and shouldn't get married. And if you're already embroiled with a cheater? Well, he shows us how to navigate that situation too, and decide whether or not a fractured relationship is worth salvaging or whether we should simply walk away. – **janandheather.com**

I was hooked on this book from the very first sample I read of it. I appreciated that Dr. Chalmer doesn't shy away from difficult topics like sex, trauma, and anxiety in relationships and that he acknowledges the difficulties those situations present in maintaining relationships. I've even recommended this book to someone for precisely that reason. **I give *Reigniting the Spark* five stars.** – **carijehlik.com**

Table of Contents

Introduction

Who Should Read This Book?

This is a book about betrayal, and how to move on from it. Not just how to move on, but how to move on with joy and gratitude. If that seems impossible, but you want to get there, you're the perfect candidate to read this book.

I've been helping people recover from betrayal for over thirty years. And I've experienced betrayal myself. I don't think I'd be nearly as effective helping people through it if I hadn't been through it myself.

Of course, anyone who's ever been in a relationship with another human being has been disappointed by someone's actions on occasion, and has disappointed others. We all let other people down sometimes, through innocent oversight, momentary selfishness, or even out-and-out hostility. I'm not talking about the small, everyday kinds of screw-ups we all experience.

No, I'm referring to the big ones. Sexual infidelity by a partner. Sexual, physical, or emotional abuse from a partner or other trusted family member. Financial malfeasance. Lying about you to others. Abandonment.

I wish I could say that those circumstances are rare. But they're not.

As you'll see, we'll also be talking about forgiveness and faith as key parts of moving on from betrayal. But let me warn you up front: If you're expecting a "faith-based" approach as that term is usually used, you're in the wrong place. As you'll know if you've read my other books, listened to the podcast I do with my wife, or seen any of my videos, I'm indeed very involved in my Jewish faith, and I'm very comfortable working with people who are active in other faiths as well. But the ideas in this book aren't specific to any particular religion, and simplistic nostrums ("Just turn it over to God", "God only gives us what we can handle", "It's all in God's plan") are ineffective, uncaring, and often insulting to someone who's experienced betrayal.

Because the reason it's so hard to heal from betrayal isn't because you don't have enough faith. Or because you're somehow not strong enough, or not mature enough. The reason it's hard to heal from betrayal is because it's hard—for lots of good evolutionary reasons. Healing doesn't happen by denying or suppressing those reasons. It happens by accepting and working with them. This book will show you how.

When you've been betrayed by someone, your relationship with them will change. Surprisingly, it can often change for the better. Sometimes changing a relationship for the better involves radical transformations such as divorce. But sometimes a betrayal can be the crisis that opens up possibilities for new levels of connection and trust within an existing relationship. And initially, it's often hard to know which way to go. Either way, this book will help you find the courage to proceed with faith in your own ability to heal. It won't be easy, but you'll come through this.

Are You Safe Enough to Focus on Healing?

One of the worst betrayals you can experience is when a trusted partner, relative, or friend threatens your physical safety. If you've been assaulted, threatened with violence, isolated from others, or otherwise prevented from acting in your own interest, then you need a safety plan. This book might be helpful to you later on, but this is not the time to worry about healing from the betrayal. Put down this book and find someone you can trust to help you get out of the situation.

Of course, even if you're not at physical risk, you might not feel emotionally safe. But read on. A lot of the work of healing from betrayal involves tolerating anxiety.

Overview of the Book

We'll start by getting to know some of the couples I've worked with over the past thirty years. These couples, and hundreds of others, have taught me more about how to work through betrayal than any of the dozens of theoretical approaches I've been trained in. By sharing their stories, I hope to share with you some of the wisdom they've taught me.

Then we'll talk about what betrayal is, and why it's so painful. That will lay the groundwork for considering forgiveness: what it's not, what it is, and whether you're ready for it. And if you are ready for forgiveness, you'll see how you might proceed, step by step.

Since forgiveness, as I describe it, involves faith, we'll talk about what faith is and is not. That will lead us to how to move on from betrayal—whether or not you want to stay with someone.

You might have noticed that I've been describing you, the reader, as someone who has experienced betrayal and wants to move on from it. I'm guessing your experience has been one in which someone else betrayed your trust. Most of the examples in the book are written from that point of view.

But if you're the person in the relationship who has betrayed another's trust, you'll benefit from this book too. I've included a chapter specifically for you as well.

Finally, we'll see what happened to those example couples we'll be following throughout the book. As we work through the ideas in this book, we'll see how those ideas came to life in those couples— for better or worse. (Yes, sometimes for worse. Nobody's ideas always work well, including mine!)

Some of the couples found forgiveness and reconciliation, and some didn't. Some of them clearly benefited from the work I did with them, and some of them didn't seem to, or had mixed results. But you'll get a sense of what can happen when people are trying to heal from betrayal, and I hope that will strengthen your faith that you can heal too.

Reflections

At the end of each chapter is a Reflections section. I urge you to give some time to the questions in those sections as you read through the book. They're designed to help you apply the ideas from the chapter to your own life, and also to set the stage for the ideas to be covered in the next chapter. When I used to teach Statistics in the 1980s (my textbook *Understanding Statistics* was published in 1986, and amazingly you can still get it from Amazon), I would introduce a new topic with exercises that led students to invent the technique about to be introduced, or at least to recognize the need for it. The Reflections sections have a similar function.

A Note to Therapists

If you're a therapist, either for individuals or for couples, I'm guessing you'll find this book both supports and challenges some of your favorite ideas about how to do this work. As I mentioned in my book *It's Not About Communication! Why Everything You Know About Couples Therapy is Wrong*, that subtitle applies to me as well. Everything *I* know about couples therapy is wrong, too!

Of course, I'm still claiming I have good ideas to offer. The problem isn't the ideas we have; it's *knowing* that our ideas are correct. When we start being loyal to our precious ideas—in other words, when our ideas become ideologies—that's when we stop hearing the people we work with, and our work does harm rather than good.

So I invite you to consider the ideas in this book in the spirit of exploration. If you find yourself questioning theoretical orthodoxy, that's probably a good thing. And if you disagree with some of my ideas, I'd love to hear about it. I sometimes disagree with my ideas too.

Chapter 1

Meet the Couples

Who Are These People?

The couples (or friends or relatives) we'll be getting to know are people I've worked with over the past 30 years of being a couples therapist. Of course, identifying details have been thoroughly disguised. If you've come to me for therapy, you might recognize a story similar to yours, but each of these couples exemplifies situations I've encountered with many other people as well.

All of the people in these couples are cis-gendered and heterosexual, as are the vast majority of the people I work with. I have worked with gay, lesbian, and trans clients, including couples, and I believe the ideas I'm offering have been helpful to them as well. But, out of respect for my own limitations, I'm leery of claims of general applicability. Much as I try to avoid "mansplaining" to women, I try to avoid "straightsplaining" to LBGTQ people.

You might want to bookmark this chapter in case you want to refresh your memory about a couple's backstory when you encounter them in later chapters. For that reason, I've arranged them alphabetically (woman's name first).

Angie and Peter

When Angie and Peter first got together, Angie was a 21-year-old senior in college, and Peter, five years older, was working as an advertising copywriter. They moved in together shortly after Angie graduated, and married a couple of years later. When I met them they had been married for 14 years, and had two sons ages 11 and 8.

When their second son was five, Peter announced that he was tired of "working for idiots" and was going to pursue a career as a freelance writer. Angie wanted to be supportive, though it meant that she had to take on evening shifts waiting tables in addition to her day job as a teacher. Meanwhile, Peter worked on a series of speculative writing projects, none of which produced an income.

After three years of working two jobs while Peter stayed home, Angie asked if he would take on some kind of job that actually made money. Peter complained that Angie was going back on her agreement to support his aspirations. He reluctantly agreed to do couples therapy only when Angie said it was either that or divorce.

At our first session, both Angie and Peter described themselves as feeling betrayed.

Beth and Albert

In his email to me asking for a couples session, Albert told me that his wife Beth had announced that she wanted to separate, after 40 years of marriage, to explore a relationship with someone at work she had become emotionally close with. Albert felt completely blindsided by this. We met for two sessions, and Beth decided to move out.

A couple of months later, Beth requested that we meet again. The man she had been involved with—sexually as well as emotionally, she now confirmed—had dumped her, at least in part because he sensed that Beth wasn't emotionally out of her marriage.

Beth realized she still loved Albert, and wanted to work on the marriage, and Albert agreed to go back to couples therapy with her.

Both Beth and Albert recognized that simply going back to how things were before was impossible. They realized that they had never let each other know about building resentments over the years, and hoped they could rebuild trust by opening up to each other.

Elsie and Charles

After 37 years of marriage, Elsie (now 58) found out that Charles (62) had been hiring prostitutes when he would travel on business, which he did frequently as he was the CEO of a large company with branches all over the country. Charles had deflected Elsie's suspicions until she found out she had contracted herpes, obviously from Charles.

At first, Charles minimized what he had done, saying he had only strayed once. But as Elsie kept pumping him for details he admitted that he had been using high-end "escort services" for the past ten years. Elsie was particularly enraged when Charles told her that he had paid extra for the "Girlfriend Experience."

At our first session Charles described himself as "the world's worst husband," and Elsie didn't disagree. But neither one wanted divorce.

Flora and Jason

I never met Jason—he was in prison the entire time I worked with Flora. When Flora first consulted me, she was 38, and had been divorced from Jason for five years. She had two children with him, ages 15 and 12.

During their ten-year marriage, Jason had violently assaulted Flora on many occasions, three of which resulted in her being hospitalized with broken bones. The first two times she convinced the hospital staff that the injuries were accidental—Jason had threatened to kill both her and the children if she told the truth. The last time, she managed to arrange for her children to be in a safe place, and she pressed charges. Jason was convicted of multiple felonies and sentenced to ten years in prison.

Flora came to me primarily for help with parenting issues. In describing her relationship with Jason, she was matter-of-fact about his continuing danger to her and the kids. She maintained a restraining order and kept a gun. But she also noted that she had long since let go of anger towards him.

Frannie and Caleb

Frannie was 45 when her father suddenly died. A couple of weeks later, she found out that her father had specifically excluded her from his will, which gave all of his estate, worth over a million dollars, to Frannie's brothers (her mother had died several years before). Although the will said merely that Frannie was to be excluded for "reasons known to her," Frannie was completely blindsided. Her father and Caleb, her husband of 20 years, had often clashed, and the only explanation that occurred to her was that her father was determined not to benefit Caleb in any way. She was devastated.

It didn't help that Frannie's relationships with her brothers were often difficult, and she didn't know how they would handle the situation. And Caleb's anger made it hard for her to talk to him about her own sense of betrayal, especially because she could see why her father had such a hard time with him.

Frannie insisted that Caleb come with her for couples therapy because she realized that this betrayal from her father was bringing longstanding tensions in her marriage to the fore.

Greta and Van

When Greta, now 50, was a 12-year-old child, her father had sexually abused her by groping her on three occasions. The first time, she told herself it was some kind of accidental touching, but the second time she realized it was intentional, and she froze with fear and confusion. The third time she pushed his hand away and ran from the room.

She didn't say anything to her mother, but from that time on, Greta avoided being alone with her father. She did tell her mother about it when Greta was 22, but her mother refused to believe it had happened the way Greta remembered it. She never talked to her father about it.

Greta married Van when she was 25 and Van was 27. Van soon noticed that Greta's relationship with her parents was strained, but didn't think much about it. Greta said simply that her parents were "difficult." Greta and Van moved to another state and would see her parents once or twice a year for brief visits. They never had children, by mutual agreement.

Now Greta's parents are both in their late 70s and still together. Her father has become frail, and her mother struggles to care for him. Greta has no siblings. Her visits to her parents have become more frequent in the past year as she tries to help them find assistance.

A few months ago Van and Greta were watching a TV movie that had a scene of a father sexually molesting his daughter. Greta started sobbing, and Van asked her what was happening. She hesitantly told him about her father's molesting her and her mother's disbelieving her.

What brought them to couples therapy? Since Greta told Van what had happened, he would become enraged when Greta said she was going to visit her parents. And his anger wasn't only directed at Greta's parents. He felt betrayed by Greta's keeping the secret from him for decades. He knew he should be supportive, but couldn't suppress his feelings of hurt, and couldn't understand why Greta would still feel an obligation to help her parents.

From Greta's perspective, Van's reaction simply reinforced the fear that had kept her from telling Van about the molestation years ago. Not only had she been betrayed by each of her parents; now she was being emotionally abandoned by her husband.

They love each other and want to stay together.

Kimberly and Matt

Kimberly and Matt, ages 34 and 35, have been together for 12 years, married for 10. They have two daughters, ages seven and four.

About six months before I met them, Matt told Kimberly he was unhappy in their marriage and said he wanted to try separating. He moved out to an apartment, had a brief sexual relationship with a woman co-worker, and then realized that he didn't want to end his marriage and wanted to move back in with Kimberly. He told Kimberly about the sexual relationship and assured her it was over. She agreed that he could move back home on the condition that they do couples therapy.

They started sessions with me shortly after Matt moved back in. After seven sessions over the course of three months, they reported that they were doing a lot better, and decided to space out their visits with me, setting up their next appointment in a month.

A few days later, Matt emailed me asking for a couples appointment as soon as possible. When we met, he tearfully said that a young woman customer of the brokerage he worked for had propositioned him for sex soon after he had moved back home, and he had agreed. They had met four or five times over two months, while he and Kimberly were doing couples therapy.

How had Kimberly found out about it? When Matt told the other woman that he wouldn't see her anymore, she got angry and sent evidence of their relationship to both Matt's boss and to Kimberly. Matt got fired from his job.

Both Kimberly and Matt say they want to save their marriage.

Lori and Phyllis

Lori and Phyllis are both in their early 50s, and have been best friends since they met in college. Shortly after they graduated they opened a boutique together selling women's clothing. Over the years their business prospered. When they consulted me they had seven locations with about 50 employees.

Their roles in the business had evolved to fit their respective strengths. Lori was the creative force, designing their storefronts, selecting the merchandise they carried, and planning promotional campaigns. Phyllis managed the financial side of the business, serving as the Chief Financial Officer of the company.

When they first came to see me, Phyllis had just told Lori that the IRS was investigating whether the two of them might be personally liable for hundreds of thousands of dollars in unpaid taxes, and had placed a lien on each of their houses. Over a five-year period, Phyllis had failed to file tax returns for the company, and didn't tell Lori about it. She assured Lori that she hadn't stolen or misallocated any of the company's money; she had simply failed to file returns and pay the company's taxes. But the IRS wasn't so sure. Lori doesn't know what to believe, and wonders what else Phyllis might have lied about.

Lori insisted on the two of them consulting a therapist together, in hopes of being able to move forward without having to dissolve their partnership. But she felt deeply betrayed. Phyllis just wanted Lori to accept her apology and move on.

Patricia and Zach

At their first session with me, Zach described himself as a sex addict, and Patricia nodded. Zach is 32 and Patricia is 34, and they've been together four years.

Zach had only recently determined that he was a sex addict, after Patricia came home early one day from work and caught him masturbating to porn. He confessed that he would watch porn and masturbate two or three times a week, and had never told Patricia about it because he knew she would be disgusted by it—which she confirmed. Patricia said she considered his behavior, both the masturbation itself and the use of porn, to be cheating. She wanted to stay with him, but only if he addressed his addiction in therapy.

Sally and Ed

Sally, age 40, came to see me with her brother Ed, 42. What brought them to therapy was a mutual desire to end estrangements that had started many years earlier.

As Sally described it, she and Ed had been each other's closest friends as children and young adults, a bond forged in the fires of abuse and neglect from their parents. Their mother was a drug addict who abandoned them when Sally was a young child. Their father kept a roof over their heads, but was also involved in the drug scene, both using and dealing. Sally was sexually abused by several of her father's customers. She cut off contact with her father as soon as she was able to get out of the house at 16, first couch-surfing at friends' houses and eventually finding a job and living on her own.

As the older brother, Ed was both supportive and protective of Sally. When he sensed that she was going down a bad path, he would take her aside and call her on it, which she came to appreciate. She was particularly grateful that Ed would never speak ill of her to anyone—she felt he was the one person in her life she could trust.

When Sally was 22, she was dating a man—we'll call him Josh—whom she didn't want to be with anymore, but didn't have the heart to break up with definitively. After months of trying to tell him it's over, she just started seeing other guys without telling him.

At the time, Ed was living in Sally's apartment. Ed decided to tell Josh what was going on. Josh called Sally in a panic and told her what Ed had told him. When Sally confronted Ed, he said he had told Josh what she was doing because it was the right thing to do.

Sally felt betrayed—how could the one person she trusted stab her in the back like that? She had Ed evicted, and refused his repeated attempts to contact her for years.

Over the years, Sally had heard that their father had managed to turn his life around, getting clean and forming a stable relationship with a woman. She had thought about contacting him, but hadn't felt ready. Ed had maintained contact with their father.

Now, 18 years after Sally had cut him off, Ed messaged Sally to tell her that their father was terminally ill. Ed was participating in his care. He hoped that Sally would want to participate too.

Sally realized she wanted to get past her sense of betrayal, but needed Ed to understand how he had hurt her. Ed wanted Sally to understand how her evicting him also felt like a betrayal. They agreed to work with a therapist in hopes of being able to work together to care for their father.

Sarah and Phil

Sarah and Phil, both in their mid-50s, have been married for 30 years. About five years ago Sarah came home from work earlier than usual and discovered Phil in their bedroom dressed in an evening gown, complete with pantyhose, bra, and high heels.

Sarah was shocked, terrified, and angry by turns. Shocked, because she had had no idea that Phil was into cross-dressing.

Terrified, because she worried that this meant that Phil was gay and would want a divorce. And angry, because she felt betrayed that Phil wouldn't have told her about his desire to cross-dress.

At first, Phil said it was a one-time thing—he had just been curious, and hadn't even thought about trying it before. Sarah tried to get past it by ignoring it. But then she started to recall some odd moments over the course of their marriage. Phil's denials didn't seem plausible. She pressed him to tell her the truth, and he finally admitted that he'd been a closeted cross-dresser since he was a teenager.

Both Phil and Sarah want to stay together. But Sarah doesn't know how to get past her sense of betrayal.

Teresa and James

Teresa and James met when they were each 26, and moved in together a few months later. They've now been together for four years.

Why are they coming to see me? James wants to get married and have a child, and Teresa is resisting both ideas. When they first got together, they hadn't talked about marriage one way or the other, but Teresa had said she was open to the idea of having a child eventually. Over the past few years, when James would bring up either the question of marriage or the question of having a child, Teresa would deflect the topic, saying she didn't want to do either until she was sure they were okay with each other.

A couple of weeks ago Teresa told James she realized she didn't want to have children, with James or anyone else. James still loves Teresa, and Teresa says she loves him and wants to stay with him. But James feels betrayed.

What Do These Couples Have in Common?

The common thread among these couples, of course, is what this book is about. Their stories are all unique, but all of them were dealing with some kind of betrayal.

What is betrayal? And why is it so painful?

Reflections on Chapter 1

1. As you've read about our example couples, I'm guessing you've thought of instances in your own life where you've felt betrayed. You've also experienced times when you've been hurt by someone important in your life, but wouldn't call it a betrayal. What's the difference? What makes some hurtful actions feel like a betrayal, and some hurtful actions not? There's no one right answer, but jot down some ideas about this.

2. I'm guessing that as you've read this chapter you've also thought of other people you know who've been betrayed one way or another. Think for a bit about their stories. You might want to jot down some notes about those stories for future reference.

3. Have you ever betrayed anyone? If so, what made it a betrayal? If not, has anyone ever accused you of betraying them, though you disagree? If so, why might they have thought it a betrayal?

Chapter 2

What is Betrayal?

Betrayal and Expectations

To betray someone is to fail, in an important way, to live up to what they expect of you based on your relationship with them.

Note the two central features of this definition.

First, the failure has to be important. Betrayal is more than simply disappointment or annoyance. My wife might be annoyed if I forget to wipe down the bathroom countertop after I brush my teeth, since I said I'd do so, but she assures me she doesn't feel betrayed. We'll have more to say about the distinction between mere annoyance and betrayal later on. I mention it here because I've worked with quite a few people who *do* report feeling betrayed when their partner simply forgets something—and when that's how they feel, it generally means something more serious is going on that they haven't been able to deal with.

Second, betrayal is based on expectations you have of a particular relationship. Our expectations of a spouse or a committed partner are different from our expectations of an adult child or parent or sibling or close friend. You can't be "betrayed" by a total stranger with whom you have no shared affinity. You can be hurt, but not betrayed.

Let's consider some of those expectations, and how they differ depending on the nature of the relationships involved.

Expectations Committed Couples Have of Each Other

For most married or otherwise committed couples in our culture, those expectations include:

- *Sexual fidelity:* In a monogamous relationship, sexual fidelity means that you don't have sex with anyone else besides your partner. Well, obviously—that's what monogamy means.

  The not-so-obvious part is that the definition of "having sex" with someone isn't what it used to be. (Again, more on that later.) *"He was sexting with someone he dated in high school. He says it's not really cheating. Sure feels like cheating to me!"*

- *Emotional fidelity:* Emotional fidelity can be even harder to pin down, but violations of it—emotional affairs—can feel like just as much of a betrayal as sexual infidelity can. *"If it was just sex, I think I could get past it. But she was looking to him for comfort, for fun, for conversation—I can't stand the way she lights up when she's texting with him."*

- *Honesty:* We expect our partners to be essentially honest with us, or at least honest about important things. Infidelity almost always involves lying, and many people have told me that the lying feels like more of a betrayal than the infidelity itself. *"I would have been angry if he had just told me he got that lap dance, but it's lying about it that makes me feel like I can't trust him anymore."*

- *Loyalty:* We want to feel that our partners are on our team, even when we screw up. If your partner speaks ill of you to others, you're apt to feel betrayed. *"I can't believe she told her parents about catching me using porn. How am I supposed to face them?"*

- *Reliability:* We expect our partners to live up to their promises and fulfill their obligations. When a partner suddenly changes the terms of the agreement we thought we had, the other partner might feel betrayed. An extreme example of this is abandonment. Addiction can also have this effect (see also "honesty"). *"He just got fired—again. I thought he was someone I could count on. If I had known he couldn't hold down a job I wouldn't have married him."*

- *Transparency:* This comes up especially in the financial life of a couple. Lots of couples operate the business aspects of their relationship with some amount of specialization—in other words, usually, one of the couple is more responsible for keeping track of their money than the other, who may or may not be more responsible for actually spending it. Whatever the arrangement, both parties generally expect that their partner will be open about what they're doing. If one of them hides a significant expenditure or liability, the other is apt to feel betrayed. *"I just found out she has a credit card I didn't know about, and there's a balance of $5000 she can't pay. What else is she keeping from me?"*

Each of the example couples we met in Chapter 1 was dealing with violations of at least one of these expectations, and some were dealing with a bunch of them. Some of the violations were obvious—for example, Charles's use of prostitutes, or Matt's cheating and lying about it in couples therapy.

But others aren't so clear-cut. Does Zach's use of porn constitute a betrayal? Patricia certainly thought so. Why was James feeling not merely hurt but betrayed by Teresa's rejection of having children? Why did Van feel betrayed by Greta's silence about her history of molestation from her father? As we'll see, healing from betrayal always involves coming to understand the expectations we have, and sometimes questioning them.

We've been talking about expectations committed partners generally have of each other. What about other relationships?

Expectations in Non-Couple Relationships

Curiously, we can use the same list. All of those expectations come up in relationships with siblings, parents, children, and even close friends—with appropriate changes based on the particular relationship we're considering:

- *Sexual fidelity:* How could sexual fidelity be an expectation in a relationship that is clearly supposed to be non-sexual?

   Anyone who's been caught cheating in a monogamous relationship has to deal not only with their partner's sense of betrayal, but also their extended family's and community's sense of betrayal. If you've cheated on your spouse, you've hurt your friends too, by hurting their loved one. And more generally, you've brought pain to your community by violating its relational ethics. We all tend to feel betrayed when someone's behavior violates community norms, even if we're not close to the person.

   Of course, another aspect of sexual fidelity in non-sexual relationships is to respect that very expectation—i.e., that the relationship is non-sexual. To sexually abuse children, or come on sexually to a friend or relative who has no interest in being sexual, is to violate that expectation.

- *Emotional fidelity:* Again, this is not as easily defined, but emotional affairs can have similar ripples in someone's wider community. Close friends can also feel betrayed by being jilted for another friend.

- *Honesty:* We expect others in close relationships to be, mostly, honest with us, though the degree to which we expect honesty varies with the particular type of relationship.

- *Loyalty:* Just as committed partners expect loyalty from each other, so do wider kinship networks, religious and cultural groups, and countries. Enemies might be viewed with fear or hatred, but betrayal is when someone from whom you expect loyalty violates that trust. We tend to treat traitors with greater contempt than we treat enemies. Prisoners of war are incarcerated and eventually repatriated, but traitors are apt to be executed.

- *Reliability:* Families expect other family members to show up at critical times. Friends expect friends to be there for them when things get tough. Employers expect employees to do their jobs, and employees expect employers to pay them and treat them fairly. Violations of these expectations can feel like betrayal.

- *Transparency:* This is an obvious expectation in a business partnership, for example. I've worked with many couples and individuals who have experienced financial betrayal from a business partner, and it's even worse when the partner is a relative or close friend.

Why Are Betrayals So Painful?

People hurt each other in all sorts of ways. What is it about betrayal that makes it so exquisitely painful?

When a new recruit goes through boot camp, they aren't surprised when the drill instructor behaves in ways that, in other settings, would be considered abusive. They might well be hurt by what the DI does. But they don't feel betrayed. They expected the DI to be that way (or should have).

Political opponents are often horrible to each other. Enemies in wars are trying to kill each other. Rival sports teams are trying to defeat each other. None of the hostile actions in those situations, hurtful though they may be, constitute betrayal. We expect adversaries to behave like adversaries. It's only betrayal when they violate the assumed rules of the game—in other words, when they violate what you expect of them.

Betrayal isn't just when someone hurts you. Betrayal is when someone important in your life hurts you when you assumed they would never hurt you that way.

It's a double-whammy: Not only are you hurt by what they did, but you're also forced to question your own judgment. *"I thought I knew you—who are you? And what other horrible surprises will happen next?"*

And the pain isn't just amplified by the surprise factor. Betrayals can involve people you've depended on for your essential safety. When someone betrays you, not only are you hurt, and have to question your own judgment; you're also faced with the loss of the relationship, and everything that goes with it. That, of course, is why betrayals by an intimate committed partner are so devastating.

Why is Sexual Betrayal So Quintessentially Painful?

I'm guessing that most of you reached out for this book because a partner cheated on you sexually. If that's not your situation, keep reading anyway! As you've already seen, I have lots of examples of other sorts of betrayal. But sexual betrayal is the most common reason couples end up in my office.

What is it about sexual betrayal that makes it the poster child for betrayal in general?

Every human culture has rules for who can have sex with whom. These rules vary with the particular culture, but there are always rules.

Some of the rules are essentially universal, holding true even in cultures that were isolated from other cultures for millennia. For example, every culture regards sex with parents and siblings as taboo. (Yes, there have been rare exceptions to the sibling rule involving certain royal dynasties—see "Game of Thrones" for a fictional example—but the rarity of those exceptions is the point.) Incest taboos make obvious evolutionary sense; when they're violated, all sorts of bad things happen both genetically and socially. People in societies that have those taboos are more likely to survive than those that don't, and they pass those taboos on to their children.

Other rules are more specific to particular cultures. For example, many cultures have allowed a man to have multiple wives—i.e., to have multiple women he supports economically and can have sex with (and children with) within the rules. But even in those cultures that allow polygamy, the vast majority of men have only one wife, mostly because they couldn't afford to support more than one.

Very few cultures have historically allowed women to have multiple male sex partners within the rules. Again, it's not hard to see the evolutionary reasons for this distinction: it's generally an advantage for a woman having a child to have help from a man, and that help is much more reliable when the man believes that the child she's having is his offspring. Since the rule against women having multiple sex partners confers a survival advantage, the rule survives.

Of course, the rules exist only because they're often violated. (No culture has a rule that says you have to breathe air, for example.) As the anthropologist Helen Fisher has pointed out, the actual sexual pairing practice our species follows can be described as "serial monogamy and clandestine adultery." Fisher explains that, in practice, adultery has evolutionary benefits too; for women, being willing to have sex with other men can mean more sources of support. But, as we noted above, having a rule against adultery (at least for women) also confers a survival benefit. So what seems to work best for a culture to survive is to have the rule *against* adultery and also *practice* adultery. It works as long as the adultery is generally kept secret—of course, that's because violations of the rule get punished.

And that's pretty much what happens, right? Whatever culture you've been raised in, you've learned rules about who's allowed to have sex with whom, and you're aware of lots of violations of those rules too. Note that this observation doesn't mean that *everyone* commits adultery; rather, it means that adultery tends to be pretty common. Maybe you've never cheated, but you definitely know people who have.

If violations of sexual taboos are so common, why is it so painful when your partner violates them? Yes, they promised you monogamy, but why should you feel so deeply betrayed when they violate that promise? Why isn't sexual cheating just one of those inevitable annoyances that go along with any relationship?

Well, I've met people where that seems to be the case. In fact, one of the characteristic differences between heterosexual couples and gay male couples is how they view sexual "straying." Note that I'm not referring to polyamory or other forms of non-monogamy here. I'm referring to couples, gay or straight, where their agreement is sexual monogamy. For many gay male couples, and even for some heterosexual couples, having sexual encounters outside the primary relationship is a violation, but doesn't necessarily rise to the level of betrayal. You talk about it and move on, much as you would if your partner spent too much money on something.

But for the great majority of the people I work with—and, I'm guessing, for you—if your partner has sex with someone else, it feels like a betrayal. Why?

I think sexual cheating feels so horrible to most of us because it threatens us on multiple levels—in other words, it feels not merely painful, but acutely dangerous. Here are some of the ways you can feel threatened when you find out your partner has been sexually unfaithful:

- Most obviously, you're confronted with the potential loss of your partner, because their having sex with someone else implies they might want to leave you to be with another who also demands monogamy.

- Losing your partner means a massive upheaval in your life. For most people, it means a loss of security, both economically and emotionally. You've built a life together. How will you cope with losing your partner? And if you're a parent of young children, how can you stand not being with your kids part of every week?

- Losing someone you love is always hard. But this loss is magnified because you're not just (potentially) losing someone you love. You're losing someone you love who is *choosing* to leave you. Which calls into question your own lovability and desirability. *"What's wrong with me that he wanted to find someone else?"*

- If you're doubting your own desirability, you're probably imagining others blaming and shaming you for not being able to keep your partner faithful. Your partner's cheating is an implicit indictment of your own value. *"How can I face my family and friends?"*

- You're not only questioning your value. You're also questioning your own judgement. *"How could I have been so blind, so gullible?"*

- If your partner says they want to stay with you, how can you risk intimacy with them, sexually or otherwise? How can you stand to have sex again when the image of your partner having sex with the other keeps intruding? And it's not just about sex—how can you believe they love you, treasure you, put you first? How can you believe anything they tell you after all the lies? *"What else was she lying to me about?"*

Sexual Betrayal and Sacredness

And there's another aspect of sexual intimacy that puts sexual infidelity in a special category.

To be sexually intimate with someone isn't just another pleasurable activity, like playing ping-pong or mahjongg. Sexual intimacy is sacred, at least for most of us.

What makes something sacred? The Latin word *sacrare*, from which the word "sacred" is derived, means to set something apart. The Hebrew word for holy, *kadosh*, has a similar meaning. When something is set apart for a particular purpose, to use it in a non-prescribed manner is to "profane" it (from Latin roots implying "outside the temple," therefore non-sacred).

Religious prohibitions of sex outside marriage, of course, are expressions of this idea. But even non-religious people usually react to violations of sexual taboos with a particular sense of disgust or outrage. That's why sex crimes are treated differently from other forms of physical violation. To label someone a sex criminal isn't merely to say they are to be feared; it's to say they're unholy and need to be shunned.

The difference between "casual" sex and sex with a committed monogamous partner is essentially the difference between the profane and the sacred. To commit to monogamy is to promise your partner that having sex has now become sacred, reserved for your relationship and no other. To violate that commitment isn't just failing to live up to a promise; it's to profane something sacred.[1]

---

[1] Nerdy note: Jonathan Haidt and his colleagues have written extensively about moral foundations theory, which describes how innate psychological systems, shaped by evolution, affect how we judge ourselves and others ethically and morally. The sense of sacredness I'm describing here fits into the "Purity" foundation. See moralfoundations.org for more on this.

If your partner has cheated on you sexually, you probably know what I'm talking about. It's not just that they've done something hurtful, or thoughtless, or dangerous to the relationship. It's that they've done something unholy.

What About Non-Sexual Betrayal?

Non-sexual betrayal can be just as threatening to a relationship as sexual betrayal. If someone you trusted has been lying to you, or hiding important information from you, or not living up to commitments to you, your fear of losing the relationship can be just as intense as if your partner had cheated sexually with someone.

Among our example couples, Frannie's sense of betrayal when she found out her father, who had just died, had disinherited her was devastating. Not only was she reeling from her father's rejection of her, but she was also facing issues in her marriage to Caleb that she had always been able to ignore. And what made this betrayal so particularly painful was that she had no chance to work it out with her father. It was hard enough to lose her father to death. But she also was forced to question what she thought she knew about his love for her.

Angie, whose husband Peter had been trying unsuccessfully to freelance for years, was questioning her trust in him when he rejected her appeal to start producing an income. James, whose partner Teresa said she didn't want children after years of saying she was open to the possibility, was left in a similar quandary. Greta was not only coping with her history of sexual abuse from her father, and her mother's dismissal of it; she was also feeling that her husband's anger at her for not telling him about it threatened their marriage. Sally was still reeling from her brother Ed's informing on her to her boyfriend 18 years before. Sarah, who found that her husband Phil was secretly into cross-dressing even before they married, was trying to sort out what to believe about his sexuality and how to cope with his keeping this secret from her for decades.

All of these betrayals had the people who had been betrayed questioning what they thought they could count on. *"Who are you? I thought I knew you!"*

However you've been betrayed, you want to heal from the pain. And since the pain of betrayal is based on violations of your expectations, a good place to start is by examining those expectations.

Reflections on Chapter 2

1. As I mentioned in the Introduction, I'm guessing that most of you reading this are reeling from some kind of betrayal. (If you're among the fortunate ones who are reading this book for other reasons, think back to situations in your own life that involved a betrayal. If you're over the age of 20, there have probably been some.)

    What about your situation feels like betrayal? What expectations were violated?
2. If your situation involves the potential loss of a relationship, what are some of the things you most fear? Some of your fears are realistic (for example, if you split up from a spouse, you'll probably have some financial pain to sort out), and some are what cognitive-behavioral therapists call "catastrophizing" (for example, no one will ever love you again). Can you tell the difference? Can you find a calm part of your psyche that can observe your panicky parts and offer some clarity?
3. If you can find that calm part, think again about the expectations that were violated in the betrayal you're dealing with. Can you think about them somewhat critically? In other words, can you let yourself speculate about whether your expectations are realistic? Or even if they're realistic, can you imagine reconsidering them

as not as necessary as you thought? (Note that giving it some thought doesn't require you to reject your values.)

Chapter 3

Are You Sure It's Really Betrayal?

Examine Your Expectations

You've been hurt, deeply. You're questioning everything you thought you knew about your relationship. You're feeling betrayed—how could someone you loved and respected do that to you?

When the specter of losing your loved one to betrayal is pushing you to panic, it's hard to consider other possibilities. But if you can find a moment of relative calm, maybe you can think about it. Betrayal is always about expectations. You can be hurt all sorts of ways by anyone, stranger or kin, but you can only be betrayed by someone if they violate what you expect of them.

Which means that if you can think about those expectations, maybe you can see the situation differently.

In other words, are you sure it's really betrayal that you experienced? Is there another way to see what happened that doesn't have to hurt as much?

Do You Have to Consider It Betrayal?

Sometimes, the answer to that question is all too simple: no, there's no other way to see what happened—at least, no other way you're willing to accept.

If a loved one physically assaults you, for example, your feeling not merely of injury but of betrayal is a necessary part of your survival mechanism. It's the feeling of betrayal that makes you re-evaluate how you think of someone.

Someone you love and trust might hurt your feelings—indeed, everyone does that from time to time. Someone you love and trust might get angry with you. But if your expectation of a loving relationship is that a lover will never cross a line into violence, then if they do so you won't just feel hurt, you'll feel betrayed—which calls your entire relationship into question. As it should. I would never advise someone to reconsider the expectation that their partner won't assault them. Maybe you'll be able to heal the relationship, but you'll need to keep the expectation that violence isn't part of it.

But other situations aren't so clear.

What Do You Mean by Monogamy?

As we discussed in Chapter 2, every culture has rules about who can have sex with whom (and, as we discussed, those rules are often violated). We'll assume your agreement with your partner is monogamy, but even if you're in a polyamorous or other non-monogamous relationship, you still have expectations about each other's sexual behavior.

So let's say you're in a monogamous relationship, which means you've agreed with your partner that neither of you will have sex with anyone else. If your partner ends up naked in bed with someone besides you, and they weren't drugged or otherwise forced to be there, it's clear they've violated the agreement. You've been betrayed by your partner. The only way you can turn this into something that isn't betrayal is to reconsider your commitment to monogamy, and even then you'll feel betrayed by your partner's failure to work that out with you first.

But let's consider Patricia and Zach from our example couples. Patricia caught Zach masturbating to porn, which he then confessed to doing several times a week. Does that violate monogamy? It did for Patricia—she said she considered Zach's behavior to be cheating. And Zach agreed with Patricia's determination that he was a "sex addict."

I've met lots of people, all of whom were women, who feel that it's cheating when their partner seeks out porn. Some people make a distinction between interacting with a person in real time (cheating) and merely watching a video (not cheating). I've met a few people, all of whom were women, who feel it's cheating when their partner masturbates by himself, and I've met lots of people, women and men, who are okay with their partner's masturbation, but not if it interferes with their sex life together.

What about other activities? I've met women who consider it cheating when their partner goes to a strip club, and I've met women who are okay with that but not okay if he gets a lap dance. I've met women who are okay with their partner getting a "happy-ending" massage, and (many more) women who are not at all okay with that.

Or consider Elsie and Charles, who were trying to stay together after Elsie found out about Charles's use of high-end "escorts" for years. Elsie was disgusted by all of it, but was particularly hurt when she found out Charles paid extra for the "Girlfriend Experience," in which the sex worker wouldn't just give him sex, but would act as if she were a committed partner during their encounter. I've met a few women over the years who (unlike Elsie) were actually okay with their partner's use of sex workers, but not okay with hiring someone to simulate a committed relationship.

Those characteristic differences I've mentioned in what women and men tend to find objectionable are probably not surprising to you, but I do want to note that they're not universal. I've met plenty of women who have no objection to porn or masturbation, for themselves or their partner. And I've met plenty of men who are bothered by their partner's showing sexual attraction to other men such as celebrities, even when there's no possibility of actually meeting them. The point is that people differ on what they are or aren't okay with from their partner, and they often don't know themselves how they feel about until they discover it.

Then there's the problem that arises when one of the partners considers the couple to be "on a break," or even broken up, and the other thinks they're still bound by a commitment to monogamy. That was the situation for Kimberly and Matt, at least initially. Matt had moved out as a trial separation, and soon began a sexual relationship with another woman. When he came back to Kimberly, he told her about the other woman. Kimberly felt it was cheating, but saw that Matt had considered them separated. Recognizing the ambiguity helped her accept what Matt had done and agree to work on the marriage.

I've met both men and women who feel betrayed when their partner "likes" or follows a past sexual partner on social media. I've met both men and women who feel betrayed when their partner's texting with someone else crosses into intimate territory, even if it's not explicitly sexual.

The point, of course, is that it's not always clear whether your partner has cheated or not—or at least, it's not always clear to both partners. You might think something is cheating that your partner thinks is allowable. A common variation of this theme is when your partner knows you disapprove of something—say, you think watching a porn video is cheating—but they disagree, so they just do it secretly. They know they're hiding something from you, but they don't think they're cheating. In fact, from your partner's perspective, you're the one with the unreasonable expectation.

The couples therapist Joe Kort notes that monogamous couples need to negotiate what they mean by monogamy, especially in the age of the internet and social media. There are ways of "having sex" with someone now that wouldn't have been conceivable outside of science fiction when I was a child. What we expect of our monogamous partners is based on assumptions that don't cover all those possibilities.

What Do You Expect in Other Relationships?

As we noted in Chapter 2, relationships with people other than monogamous partners also involve expectations. But, just as in monogamous relationships, the devil is in the details.

For example, consider what we expect from our parents. The expectation that parents won't sexually abuse their children, and will help them if someone else does, is hardly controversial. But I've met many survivors of childhood abuse, like Greta from our example couples, who still maintain relationships with the parents who abused them. Even though Greta felt betrayed by her father's molestation and her mother's denial, she also recognized that (unlike many survivors) she had been able to protect herself from further incidents. In other words, there are gray areas of betrayal—it's not black-and-white. And she felt an obligation to assist her parents as they age, in spite of their inadequacies.

Rules Aren't the Solution

Betrayal is based on expectations. That means that if you talk to your partner before you do something that you have reason to think will cross your partner's line—in other words, if you make sure you're clear about each other's expectations and behave accordingly—you'll avoid betraying each other. Make it a rule you agree on: if in doubt, talk about it. Simple, right?

Well, no.

Of course, if I'm worried that my partner is not okay with something I'm thinking about, I can ask. *"Is it okay with you if I go with the guys to the strip club?"* *"How would you feel if I have lunch with my ex-boyfriend?"* Be clear about where each other's red lines are, and then you can stay on the right side of them.

But the problem is that you can't always know for sure exactly where your partner's red lines are—or your own red lines, for that matter. What if you don't realize something might cross a line until you've crossed it, or your partner has?

And what if you're afraid to bring it up, because even bringing it up might cross a line? Lots of couples avoid bringing up topics they worry will just result in a nasty fight without resolution. And this phenomenon is particularly insidious, because it can happen without either party being fully aware of it.

No set of rules will protect you from the possibility that you'll violate each other's expectations—because *expectations are fluid*. Things you or your partner might have rejected at one time might be okay now, or vice versa. And you can't always tell in advance.[2]

---

[2] For more on this, see my book *It's Not About Communication!*, in which I expand on the idea that rules—even rules based on good ideas—won't help.

If rules won't protect you, how can you be sure you won't be betrayed?

The answer—and it's not an easy one—is that *you can't*. Even a loving, well-meaning partner could betray you. And to get through it, you'll have to be willing to look critically at your own expectations.

Are Your Expectations Realistic?

Let's look at some situations that might invite you to reconsider your expectations. First, let's consider whether your expectations are realistic.

As I mentioned in Chapter 2, I've met people who feel betrayed when their partner simply forgets to do something they promised to do. If that's you, you'll never have a relationship in which your partner doesn't betray you. And if that's your partner, you'll betray your partner sooner or later—probably sooner, and often. In other words, if your expectation from your partner is that they'll never screw up by forgetting something, you've set an impossible standard. They'll forget things. You'll forget things. I'll forget things. Expecting otherwise is just unrealistic.

Okay, that's obvious to most people. But what about the expectation that your partner will never lie to you? Or never hide something from you? Or never say something unkind to you?

Everyone is a liar. Yes, that includes you. And me. We're all a bunch of liars. We shape our descriptions of reality to fit our needs. If you don't believe that, you're lying to yourself.

I don't mean to dismiss the moral implications of lying to someone. On the contrary, lying can be a deeply hurtful offense, rising to the level of a deal-breaker. And it's generally a bad idea in any relationship, especially close ones. I don't recommend it!

But I'm just saying that the circumstances matter. I'm saying that an expectation that someone in your life will never lie to you—

meaning that lying to you constitutes a betrayal, regardless of the circumstances—is setting yourself up for failure.

Of course, one of the main reasons we lie is to avoid the consequences of telling the truth. We lie to stay out of trouble. Your partner could lie to you about whether they ate an extra cookie, and they could lie to you about whether they slept with their co-worker. Someone lying about the cookie isn't necessarily more likely to lie about the co-worker. They're radically different circumstances.

And there are degrees of wrongdoing. It's not black-and-white. I've met lots of people who think that *any* evidence of lying means they can't trust their partner about anything. That's just not realistic. If you believe that, you're setting yourself up for a world of relationship problems.

Similarly, there are degrees of severity for unkindness, or deviousness, or unreliability. There are even degrees of severity for violations of monogamy. Flirting with someone else can feel disrespectful to a partner, but it's not the same as making out with someone, or having a one-night stand, or having a months-long affair. There are degrees.

Recognizing those degrees, and examining your expectations about them, doesn't presuppose what you'll find acceptable or not. You might recognize, for example, that your partner's drunken make-out session wasn't the same as a full-blown love affair, but still conclude that you don't want to be with someone who would ever stray in that way. But if you're willing to look critically at your own expectations, you might find you can talk about what happened without dissolving into either rage or panic. And that's the beginning of healing.

Could You Reconsider Your Values?

You've been betrayed. And you've determined that your expectations are realistic—in other words, you're not expecting the impossible.

You recognize that we're all fallible, and you're not trying to hold your partner to a standard of perfection. Now what?

Well, you could end the relationship. Or you could work with your partner to see if they could give you reason to believe they can meet your expectations going forward. And we'll address both of those possibilities in later chapters, when we talk about forgiveness and moving on.

But before you proceed, it's worth checking another possibility.

Remember Patricia and Zach? They came to their first session convinced that Zach was a "sex addict" because he had the habit of masturbating to porn several times a week. Patricia was disgusted by Zach's behavior, and only found out about it because she came home unexpectedly.

She was appalled by his using porn, which she considered immoral. She was insulted by his masturbating at all, which she considered a form of cheating—if he's having sex, it's supposed to be with her. And she considered his secrecy about it to be confirmation that he knew it was wrong. The only way she could imagine staying together was to view his behavior as something he couldn't control on his own—an addiction—which allowed for the possibility that it could be treated.

From Patricia's point of view, her expectations weren't unrealistic. Lots of people—especially in particular religious communities—view both porn and masturbation as sinful, and strive to avoid them. The fact that many people violate those expectations doesn't make the expectations unrealistic. Many people violate monogamy, but many people are faithful to it; an expectation of monogamy doesn't always work, but it's not an inherently unrealistic expectation. That can be true of an expectation that someone in a relationship won't use porn, and won't masturbate.

I don't tell people what they should accept or not, and I didn't do that with Patricia and Zach. In that respect, I differ from a lot of conventional wisdom that says that what Patricia and Zach need is "psychoeducation." If I used the psychoeducational approach, I might tell them that masturbation is a healthy part of sexual expression, and cite data on how prevalent it is. In effect, I'd tell Patricia her expectations *are* unrealistic.

The reason I don't set out to "educate" people who consult me is that I genuinely don't think I know better than they do. My expertise is about helping *them* figure out what to do, not telling them what to do. It's not that I don't have my own opinions—in fact, I agree with the idea that masturbation can be a healthy part of anyone's sex life. And I'm happy to offer my opinion in the conversation.

But I'm also aware that my opinions come from my life experience and frames of reference—and other people have their own. To assert that my opinions are necessarily better than theirs is not only arrogant; it's also ineffective. If I'm trying to sell someone my point of view, I'm not actually listening to them.

So I don't tell anyone *what* to think.

But I do suggest that whatever they think, it's worth taking a second look—because sometimes we change our minds. And even if we don't change our minds completely, just raising the question can open up possibilities for mutual understanding.

For example, was it possible that Patricia could reconsider how she viewed Zach's masturbating? Rather than automatically consider it cheating, could she consider other possibilities? Could she be curious about how Zach viewed it?

For many people, masturbation is simply a pleasant release. Yes, some people's masturbation habits can be problematic, especially if they turn to masturbation as a way of avoiding sex with their partner. And yes, frequent use of porn can also be problematic, particularly in terms of how it can lead to dependency on porn for sexual arousal, to the detriment of having sex with an actual person.

But do you have to view a partner's masturbation as cheating? Zach didn't think he was cheating on Patricia. For Zach, like the vast majority of men, being turned on by sexually-oriented images was part of his erotic orientation. Bringing himself to orgasm was something he had done regularly since he first figured out how to do it as a young teenager. And as we talked about it, he started to question whether describing himself as a "sex addict" was useful.

As Patricia thought about it and heard Zach's thoughts, she realized that her main problem wasn't that Zach was masturbating. She knew that most men and women masturbate on occasion, even if they're partnered. And she wasn't coming from a fundamentalist religious perspective. She was willing to think about the nuances.

No, her main problem was that she felt that his masturbating, especially while he was looking at images of other women, meant that she wasn't enough for him. She felt there must be something lacking in her if he was turned on by thoughts of other women. The women in the porn she saw him viewing didn't look like her. That's why it felt like cheating—he was lusting after some other kind of woman, and there was no way she could compete with that.

Zach assured her that he loved and desired her, but Patricia couldn't reconcile his reassurance with what she saw. And what about their sex life with each other? Why wasn't it enough for him? That question led them to think about their intimacy in general. How had they ended up where they are?

Notice how simply questioning the assumption that masturbation and porn use was cheating opened up a conversation about what was actually happening in their relationship. This didn't require that either Patricia or Zach reject how they felt about it; it just required that they be willing to look past their initial reactions.

I mentioned earlier that no fixed rules or agreements with your partner will completely protect you from the possibility of being betrayed. And I can say the same of fixed values. Values, principles, ethical guidelines, religious commandments, laws—all of these are vital parts of human culture. Without them, we'd be in a Hobbesian nightmare.[3] But rigid, uncompromising adherence to rules and laws without regard to extenuating circumstances also leads to a nightmare, in which we're so bound by our preconceptions that we can't move towards healing.

Even if we don't end up changing our values or expectations, the process of questioning them can open pathways to mutual understanding, as it did for Patricia and Zach.

How Do You Heal the Pain?

You've considered your expectations. They're not unrealistic. And you've carefully examined your values, not just as abstract principles, but in the context of your actual situation.

And you're still feeling betrayed.

How can you begin to heal? How do you move past the anger, self-doubt, shame, and fear of what lies ahead? How do you decide what to do about the relationship?

And how do you let go, so you're no longer overwhelmed by the pain of it all?

As we'll see, getting to that level of acceptance, where you're no longer overwhelmed by the pain, is what I mean by forgiveness. In other words, forgiveness is healing.

Reflections on Chapter 3

1. Think about a time when you experienced betrayal, especially if it's long enough ago that you've matured a lot since then. Think

---

[3] Hobbes was the philosopher who described human nature as such that life without socially-enforced restrictions would be "solitary, poor, nasty, brutish, and short."

particularly about the expectations you had that were violated in the betrayal. What were they? Have you reconsidered any of those expectations since then?

2. If you're in a monogamous relationship, have you talked to your partner about just what that means? Have you had situations arise that were in a gray area—say, texting with a friend that veered into more intimate topics, or internet activities that one of you found close to the line? If you've talked about it, how did it go? If you haven't talked about it, why not?

3. Have you experienced betrayal in non-couple relationships—say, from a parent or sibling or close friend? If so, what expectations of yours were violated? Have you reconsidered any of those expectations since the betrayal?

4. Think about a time someone close to you hurt you. This could be something you consider a betrayal, but it could also be something that didn't rise to the level of betrayal. Are you still angry about it when you're reminded of it? If so, have you wondered if you could release yourself from the anger?

5. If you're still angry about a time someone hurt you, do you blame yourself for not preventing it? Do you blame the person who hurt you?

6. If you're not still angry about a time someone hurt you, how did you get past the anger? Do you recall a particular time when you let go of the anger, or did time seem to take care of it on its own?

7. If you've been able to get past the anger, did the person who hurt you help with that, perhaps by apologizing? Can you think of times you've been able to get past the anger even if the person who hurt you didn't acknowledge what they did?

Chapter 4

What Is Forgiveness?

What Isn't Forgiveness?

As I mentioned at the end of Chapter 3, forgiveness is about healing from the pain of a betrayal. But I realize people use the word forgiveness in a variety of ways, and what I'm talking about isn't the same as some of those ways. In fact, I think some of the ways the term gets used are actually harmful.

We'll get to what I mean by forgiveness. But let's start by talking about what forgiveness is *not,* at least as I use the term.

Forgiveness Doesn't Minimize What Happened

If I forgive someone who hurt me, that doesn't mean I now consider what they did to be no big deal.

Of course, there are situations where you might well reconsider how bad you thought something was. Maybe, with time, you can recognize that your standards for judging what someone did were too harsh. Maturity has a way of offering some perspective.

Maybe that time when someone didn't show up for a date wasn't the huge betrayal you thought it was when you were sixteen. Maybe you can see that your anger about it was misplaced, especially after the twenty-fifth reunion when you find out that they had left you a note telling you they couldn't come, which you never got, and they wondered why you were so cold to them after that, but then they moved away. (No, that's not an actual story I've heard, but I've known people with similar stories who have held grudges that long.)

And there are situations where you come to recognize that you were to blame too—that it wasn't all one way. Again, with maturity comes perspective. In hindsight, you can let go of your harsh judgement.

But then there are those situations where you still consider what someone did to have been really, really bad. Bad like sexual abuse. Bad like drunk driving resulting in killing a loved one. Bad like abandoning you and leaving you broke.

I'm saying it's possible to forgive someone even in those situations. You don't have to minimize or moderate your view of what they did to be able to forgive someone.

Moreover, forgiving someone doesn't mean that you absolve them of responsibility for what they did. You might still pursue compensation or other forms of accountability. You can forgive someone and still testify against them in a trial. You can forgive someone and still sue them for damages. You can forgive someone and still divorce them.

Forgiveness Isn't Forgetting

The idea of "forgive and forget" is utter nonsense.

Forgiveness is about letting go of the residual anger and pain. It's not about forgetting what happened.

There are good reasons why we *don't* forget about bad things that happen to us—even after we're able to let go of the pain. Forgiving someone doesn't mean they're safe to be around.

More generally...

Forgiveness Doesn't Mean Trust

You can forgive someone and still not trust them.

Consider Flora, who had forgiven her ex-husband Jason. Jason had violently put her in the hospital on multiple occasions until she was finally able to escape. Forgiveness meant that she no longer thought of him with anger. She could even appreciate the good times they had had together. But she maintained a restraining order against him, and kept a gun nearby which she was prepared to use if he showed up after he got out of prison. She had no reason to think he was any less dangerous than he was before.

In other words, forgiveness doesn't make you stupid.

Forgiveness Doesn't Require Remorse from the Betrayer

Flora also exemplified another interesting possibility: You can forgive someone who shows no sign of remorse or repentance.

This distinction is where different understandings of forgiveness diverge. That's especially true when you think about forgiveness from the point of view of someone who wants to be forgiven. If I ask you to forgive me after I've hurt you, I'm implicitly asking you to extend kindness to me—isn't that what forgiveness means? And if you forgive me, you'll let me back into your good graces, and we can pick up where we left off, right? That's a tall order if I haven't shown you genuine remorse.

We'll talk more about that in Chapter 13 when we focus on how to move on from a betrayal.

For now, the point is that you can forgive someone even if they haven't shown remorse. Genuine remorse is a precondition for trust—how can I believe someone won't do the same thing if they don't feel bad about having done it? But I could still let go of my anger—to forgive—much as Flora was able to. As we noted, you can forgive someone you don't trust at all.

And the converse is also true: Someone could show genuine remorse well before you're able to forgive them. Remorse doesn't guarantee forgiveness, and its absence doesn't preclude it.

Someone expressing remorse for hurting you is hoping you'll forgive them. But whether or not you forgive them isn't determined by how sorry they are.

If you're starting to get the idea that forgiveness isn't actually about the person who hurt you, you're right. Read on!

Forgiveness Doesn't Mean Restoring the Relationship

This is a corollary to the idea that you can forgive someone you don't trust. Just because you've forgiven someone doesn't mean that you're willing to restore the relationship to what it was.

I've already noted that you can forgive someone but still split up with them. Of course, you can also forgive someone and decide to stay with them. The other two cells of the two-by-two table are also available: You can stay angry at someone (i.e., not forgive them) and split up, and you can stay angry at someone and stay together. I especially don't recommend that last option, but I've met lots of couples in that situation.

The one option you don't have, though, is to forgive someone and then go back to just how things were before.

You can try to pretend that nothing has changed, but you'd be deluding yourself and each other. When therapists tell you to make a rule with your partner that says, "No bringing up the past," they're basically telling you to ignore reality. It doesn't work.

No, when there's been a betrayal, the relationship will change. What you hope, of course, is that it will change for the better. That may or may not mean staying together, or even staying in contact.

What Is Forgiveness?

We've talked about a bunch of things that forgiveness is not. It's not minimizing what happened, or absolving someone of responsibility. It's not forgetting what happened. It's not the same as trusting someone, or restoring your relationship with them to what it was, no matter how remorseful they are.

Then what *is* forgiveness?

Forgiveness is when you are no longer preoccupied with your anger and hurt from what someone did to you. You remember how you felt, and you might still feel some of it. But you're no longer preoccupied with it. It no longer haunts you.

To forgive someone means that you *were* hurt by what they did, but you've recovered from it. If you weren't hurt, of course, there's nothing to forgive.

Forgiveness from betrayal means that when you're reminded of what happened, you can think about it without descending into panic.

It won't be a pleasant memory, but it won't ruin your day either. You won't be "triggered" by a reminder of what happened, which is to say your brain/body won't respond as if you're in imminent danger. The betrayal will be a memory, not a present threat.

In effect, you've forgiven someone when you no longer experience a big, nasty reaction when you think about them. That big, nasty reaction—be it anger, fear, crushing sadness, grief, whatever—is essentially a form of panic. When you no longer panic when you're reminded of the betrayal, you've forgiven the betrayal.

Forgiveness is an Inside Job

I mentioned above that forgiveness, as I'm describing it, isn't about the person who hurt you. You can forgive someone, or not, regardless of what they did and what they've said about it.

Forgiveness isn't about anyone else. It's about you.

When you've forgiven, you're essentially free of the anger, resentment, and panic. You can think clearly about what happened and make well-informed decisions about how to handle it.

As many people, especially in recovery, have said, forgiveness is an inside job.

Forgiveness and Trauma

If you're familiar with how people recover from post-traumatic stress disorder (PTSD), you'll recognize a similarity with the process of forgiveness. In fact, getting to forgiveness from a betrayal is essentially the same thing as recovering from any sort of serious trauma. It's a learning process. Your brain needs to learn that the *memory* of the trauma isn't itself dangerous.

You learn this the way you learn pretty much anything: by repetition—not repetition of the trauma itself, but repetition of the *memory* of the trauma. If you're able to think about what happened and still feel basically safe, you'll learn not to fear the memory. All of the therapeutic modalities that have been shown to be effective for PTSD involve some sort of exposure to the memory coupled with a setting of basic safety. Even drug-assisted therapies such as ketamine or psychedelic microdosing seem, as far as I can tell, to be allowing your brain to learn that the memory of what happened is okay to visit without clicking into fight, flight, or freeze.

Getting to forgiveness after a betrayal involves the same process, whether or not you need therapeutic help. You need healing experiences, in which you can think about the betrayal, as bad as it was, without your brain trying to escape the thought.

How do you give yourself those healing experiences? We'll get into that in Chapter 7. And we'll see that a mindset of faith is central to forgiveness—more on that in Chapter 12.

But first, let's consider whether you should even try to forgive. Because there are good reasons to forgive—but as we'll see in Chapter 6, there are also circumstances where trying to forgive actually makes things worse.

Reflections on Chapter 4

1. How do you think of forgiveness? Think of a time when you've been able to forgive a hurt. What practical difference did forgiveness make in how you felt? What difference did it make in your relationship to whoever hurt you?
2. I said in this chapter that forgiveness is an "inside job," meaning that you can forgive someone you still don't trust, someone who shows no remorse, and someone who you aren't willing to stay together with. Does that idea work for you? (Feel free to disagree with me!) Have you ever been able to forgive someone who didn't apologize or even acknowledge that they hurt you?

3. Whether or not you like the idea of forgiveness as an inside job, what difference does it make to think of it that way? In other words, if you feel it's possible to forgive someone regardless of their attitudes or actions, how might that affect you? Conversely, if you feel you can't forgive someone who doesn't show they deserve forgiveness, how might that affect you?

4. Why even try to forgive a betrayal? I've guessed that most of you are reading this book because you've been betrayed. What do you hope will feel better for you as you heal from the betrayal? How does forgiveness fit into that healing? Imagine how you'll feel when you've healed. What will be different for you?

Chapter 5

Why Forgive?

Forgiveness Frees You from a Heavy Burden

When you forgive someone who betrayed you, you're free of the burden of anger, resentment, and bitterness. Reminders of the betrayal are no longer dangerous to you, so you no longer have to avoid situations that remind you. You can get on with your life.

That's why you should forgive. When you forgive, you're free.

Notice that the person who hurt you is not involved in the question of whether to forgive. It's not about them. The decision to forgive is about you. As we said in Chapter 4, forgiveness is an inside job.

When you've forgiven a betrayal, you're no longer pushed into panic when you're reminded of it. That means you can think clearly about how you want to handle your relationship with the person who betrayed you. You get your brain back.

As we'll see in Chapter 6, just because forgiving has benefits doesn't mean you're ready to forgive. There are circumstances in which you *need* the anger. But eventually, the way of forgiveness is the way of freedom.

Forgiving the Unforgivable

Wait a minute. It's one thing to imagine forgiving someone who insulted you, or even cheated on you. But what about acts of sheer, unmitigated evil?

I'm Jewish. How can I forgive Hitler for murdering millions of my people? How can I forgive the Nazis for going along with him?

Aren't some betrayals simply unforgivable?

That depends on what you mean by forgiveness.

If forgiveness means freedom from the burden of anger and panic when you're reminded of the betrayal, then *anything* is forgivable—because forgiveness isn't about what someone else did, or whether or not they apologized. It's about your own reactions. Forgiveness is a form of healing. Again, it's an inside job.

I don't have to fly into a rage when I think about Hitler, or the virulent antisemitism that continues to manifest itself today. In fact, flying into a rage doesn't help, unless I'm being actively attacked, and even then rage can cloud my thinking and make me less effective, not more.

Which means that I *can* forgive Hitler and the Nazis—and still be clear that I would oppose what they stood for in whatever way I deem necessary, including war. I'm certainly not going to forget what they did, much less condone it or minimize it. But I can still forgive. Forgiveness isn't about them. It's about my own ability to get past the panic reaction.

Viktor Frankl was a psychiatrist who survived Auschwitz, and yet was able to forgive in the sense I'm talking about. His book *Man's Search for Meaning* is an account of his experiences and how he was able to retain his moral clarity without succumbing to despair.

You may not be dealing with a betrayal on the level of the Holocaust. But I don't want to minimize the pain you're going through. When someone betrays you, the shock, anger, and grief can seem insurmountable. Maybe your whole life has been pushed into terrifying uncertainty. It's not small, even if it isn't Auschwitz.

What I'm saying is that the magnitude of the betrayal doesn't determine whether or not it's possible to forgive.

It's Not Just Semantics

I'm saying you can forgive *anything*, at least in theory, because forgiveness doesn't mean suspending your moral judgment, and forgiveness doesn't determine how you handle your relationship with someone who hurt you.

Couldn't you say I'm just messing with semantics? When you say you can't forgive your unrepentant ex-spouse, meaning you won't get back together with them, isn't that a common understanding of what forgiveness means? When you say you can't forgive someone who embezzled from your business, meaning you won't continue to employ them, doesn't that sound reasonable?

And when you say you can't forgive Nazis, meaning you're morally appalled at the sheer evil of what they did, and can never justify it or explain it away, doesn't that make sense?

Well, sure. Lots of people think of forgiveness as describing how you relate to the one who hurt you, not just about the state of mind of the person doing the forgiving. In that sense, forgiveness *isn't* just an inside job.

The reason I'm insisting on defining forgiveness as an inside job is simple: that idea empowers you.

And the other way—thinking of forgiveness as depending on what the person who hurt you does or doesn't do—disempowers you.

If you think of forgiveness as contingent on someone else, you're depriving yourself of the power to heal. If you can't let go of the anger and pain because of what someone else is or isn't doing, you're ceding your power to them. As Viktor Frankl noted, even when you can't control circumstances, the one thing you can control is how you respond to them.

Remember Greta, who had been sexually abused by her father as a child? She had never discussed it with her father, and had no expectation that he would ever acknowledge what he had done, much less apologize for it.

Or consider Flora, whose ex-husband never expressed the slightest remorse for his violence toward her. Neither Greta nor Flora had any illusions about whether they could consider the person who hurt them to be safe. Neither Greta's father nor Flora's ex-husband "deserved" forgiveness if you think of forgiveness as contingent on someone's accepting responsibility for what they did.

It would have been easy for Greta and Flora to attribute their continued traumatization to their abusers' lack of remorse.

But both Greta and Flora realized that healing was their own responsibility. In other words, they recognized that they could free themselves of the burden of being preoccupied or triggered. And no one else—not even the one who hurt them—could do it for them.

Which is how I define forgiveness. Greta and Flora realized they could forgive the unforgivable—because forgiveness isn't about anyone else.

Let's review what we talked about in Chapter 4 about what forgiveness is *not*. Forgiving someone doesn't mean that you minimize what they did. You can still prosecute, sue, or divorce someone you've forgiven. Forgiveness doesn't mean forgetting. Forgiving someone doesn't mean you can trust them, or that you agree to restore your relationship with them to what it was.

For people like Greta and Flora, forgiveness didn't make them less safe in their dealings with their abusers. On the contrary, their ability to think clearly, without panic, made them safer.

As Anne Lamott put it, "not forgiving is like drinking rat poison and then waiting for the rat to die." Forgiveness gets the poison out of you. Then you can deal with the rat.

Reflections on Chapter 5

1. I'm claiming that you can forgive *anything*, at least if you think of forgiveness the way I've described it, as an inside job. How does that idea strike you? Are there things that simply ought to be unforgivable? Maybe I *should* feel rage when I'm reminded of some heinous betrayals. What do you think?

2. When a white supremacist murdered nine people in a church in Charleston, South Carolina in 2014, many of the victims' relatives who came to the shooter's bond hearing, only two days after the shooting, said that they forgave him. What do you think they meant by that? Do you believe that they could let go of anger that quickly? What might have made that possible for them?

3. Are there times when forgiveness is a bad idea? In other words, are there times when you might need to stay angry, at least for a time?

Chapter 6

When You Shouldn't Forgive

You Might Not Be Ready to Forgive

Let's put in a word for *not* forgiving.

The reactions of shock, disbelief, and anger you felt when you realized you've been betrayed are normal, not pathological. You weren't crazy to feel the way you felt. Each of those reactions has an evolutionary basis. They exist to help us survive.

I'm not denying that people *can* be crazy sometimes. If you're convinced the FBI is controlling your thoughts because you can hear them talking to you, and you see your partner's actions as part of the conspiracy, you're dealing with a brain malfunction. (And I doubt you'd be reading this book.) If so, your reactions are out of touch with reality. You don't need to forgive; you need to get your schizophrenia treated, and then you can worry about forgiving.

But that's not you. Your reactions were what healthy brains do in the circumstances you were presented with. Your brain/body/mind is trying to protect you. The same is true, incidentally, for PTSD: the hyper-alertness, tendency to flashbacks, and susceptibility to triggers that characterize PTSD are all manifestations of a healthy brain trying to protect someone from further disaster.

In other words, you *need* some of those reactions, at least for a time.

Once you're past the initial shock and disbelief, you're confronted with a situation that needs action. Someone has betrayed you. Now what?

Forgiveness is about letting go of anger. But what if you need the anger?

Maybe You Need to Stay Angry

Anger is a powerful motivator. It's a message from your body that says, powerfully, "Change this!"

If you're being abused by someone, it's all too easy to blame yourself, which can mean denying, minimizing, or even justifying what they're doing.

I've met many people who were unable to escape abusive partners until the partner did something that threatened their child— at which point their rage overcame their fear and they were able to act decisively.

If you're still being hurt, forgiveness is premature. You need the anger to get out of the situation.

Even when you're relatively safe, no longer being hurt by whoever betrayed you, you might still need to feel anger at that person. As we'll discuss in Chapter 9, an essential part of forgiveness is to forgive yourself for not preventing what happened. And just as anger motivates you to get out of an intolerable situation, anger at whoever betrayed you can protect you from blaming yourself for things that weren't your fault.

In other words, anger directed outward is often a necessary part of healing from trauma.

You've probably heard of the five stages of grief described by Elisabeth Kübler-Ross: denial, anger, bargaining, depression, and acceptance. To recover from betrayal is a form of working through grief. Anger is a part of the process. To try to deny it—that is, to try to forgive when you still need the anger—doesn't free you; it just keeps you stuck.

Of course, *how* you handle your anger is still your own responsibility. No matter how justifiable your anger is, and no matter how much you may need it as part of your recovery from the betrayal, you're still responsible for how you express it. It won't help your recovery to act abusively yourself.

How you handle your anger is especially important if you have hope of staying in a relationship with the person who betrayed you. If your anger at your partner's betrayal leads you to betray them in turn, you're just perpetuating the cycle. When I meet a couple who are angry with each other—which is more the norm than the exception at a first session—both feel their anger is justified. They both have iconic examples readily available to cite when they're explaining why they have every reason to be angry.

Working toward forgiveness isn't about denying or minimizing the reasons you're angry. It's about recovering from the trauma, so you can see what happened in all its complexity rather than instantly clicking into defensive mode.

You can't simply dismiss your anger. It's part of healing. And until you can work through it, you're not ready to forgive.

No One Else Can Determine How You Should Feel

The central idea of this book is that forgiveness is good. Forgiveness is how you free yourself. Forgiveness is essential to recovering from betrayal.

But, as we've just discussed, that doesn't mean you're ready to forgive.

We'll talk in Chapter 7 about how you can decide when you're ready to forgive. For now, I just want to acknowledge what you've probably already encountered. Lots of well-meaning people—friends, family, clergy, therapists, even authors of books on betrayal and forgiveness—might be telling you how you should feel.

Maybe they're urging forgiveness. People who care about you see how much pain you're in, and urge you to get past it.

The problem with pushing you to forgive when you're not ready is that it doesn't work. You won't be free—you'll just suppress how you feel. I've met quite a few women who've been urged to forgive their cheating partner by parents or in-laws so as not to break up the family. I've also met women who've been told by their pastors to return to abusive husbands and submit themselves.

Urging someone to forgive while they're still being abused is basically criminal—it abets the abuse.

Or if friends and loved ones are not urging forgiveness, they might be urging the opposite reaction—perhaps revenge or ostracization or public shaming of the betrayer. Social media are very effective ways of promoting someone's cancellation.

Curiously, urging you to feel and act on your anger doesn't help either. Your friends might be angry themselves at the betrayer—after all, in hurting you the betrayer hurt someone they care about. So it's not surprising that they might encourage your anger, especially if they've been betrayed in similar ways themselves.

But pushing you to be angry doesn't work any better than pushing you to forgive. It just distracts you from what you need to figure out. And your friends' encouragement of your anger, however well-meaning, can deprive you of what you really need, which is empathetic support for you as you are.

Remember Elsie and Charles? Elsie told me that she hadn't told anyone about Charles's use of prostitutes, and felt completely isolated in her anger and pain. What stopped her was her worry that her friends would shame her for staying in the marriage, rather than empathize with her struggle to heal. Her worry felt realistic to her especially because she herself had reacted similarly when a close friend told her about being cheated on.

A friend of mine tells a similar story about consulting her minister for help dealing with her husband's infidelity. She hadn't told anyone, and was trying to find a way to save the marriage because she didn't know how she would be able to support herself and her young children if they split up. She told the minister that she wanted to find a way to get past the anger. His response was to tell her she had to divorce—that, in effect, she was crazy to want to find a way to save the marriage. My friend found this advice worse than unhelpful. Even though she eventually did go on to divorce her husband, the minister's advice didn't help her reach that conclusion—it simply reinforced her sense of isolation.

If you've been betrayed you're having enough trouble trying to sort out your feelings and decide what to do. Unfortunately, you also have to cope with other people's opinions too, or risk isolating yourself. If you have a friend or two—and maybe a clergyperson or therapist—who actually listens to you rather than telling you how you should react, you're lucky indeed. (And if you *are* one of those friends, there's a special place in heaven for you.)

You can't determine how your friends and family will react. But your healing will depend on your understanding that you're responsible for your own choices. You're entitled to make those choices whether or not your friends approve.

The Betrayer Can't Determine When You're Ready to Forgive

And it's not just friends and loved ones and advisors who may be urging you to forgive. What about the person who betrayed you?

When someone betrays you, they almost always want you to forgive them.

Of course, there are exceptions. In particular, if the betrayer doesn't think what they did was a betrayal, they won't want your forgiveness; they'll just want you to recognize that they're right and you're wrong. Flora's ex, Jason, showed no signs of considering his violence to have been a betrayal—he seemed to think Flora had it coming. As far as she could tell he was an irredeemable jerk. She didn't have to worry about his desire for forgiveness because there wasn't any.

But suppose you want to heal a relationship with someone who betrayed you. Consider Kimberly and Matt, the couple who had separated and reunited, after which Matt was caught cheating with a customer who then told Kimberly about it and also got Matt fired. Both Kimberly and Matt wanted to find a way to save their marriage.

Matt, of course, was desperately hoping that Kimberly could forgive him. And Kimberly also wanted to find a way to forgive Matt. They had built a life together, and she didn't want to lose it. And she still loved Matt.

But Matt's frequent requests for reassurance from Kimberly were getting in the way of her actually being able to forgive him. She was angry, and no matter how much Matt expressed his remorse, she wasn't going to be able to let go of that anger until she felt ready.

Part of Kimberly's anger was that she didn't believe Matt's remorse—or more precisely, she felt that his remorse was more about getting caught than about what he got caught doing. She could believe that he loved her in spite of cheating on her. She could even believe that he sincerely intended to remain faithful to her. But she couldn't believe that he had learned what he needed to learn so that she could trust that intention. He just seemed to think they could go back to where they were before he cheated. Her anger protected her from entertaining that comfortable illusion herself.

Whether or not you're ready to forgive, how can you get through the pain? If you're not ready to forgive, how do you cope with the anger and anguish? And how can you heal from the panic enough that you might be able to consider forgiving?

Those are the subjects of Chapter 7.

Reflections on Chapter 6

1. If you're reading this because you've been betrayed and want to heal, where are you on the journey? In particular, do you feel ready to forgive? Or are you in a situation where you are still being hurt, and need to focus on getting out of it before you can think about forgiving?
2. Have you talked about the betrayal with people close to you, or people who advise you such as a therapist or clergyperson? If not, why not?
3. If you have talked with others about the situation, what did you find helpful or unhelpful?
4. Has the person who hurt you asked for forgiveness? If so, were you ready to offer forgiveness? Have you had experiences like Kimberly had, in which the betrayer's requests for forgiveness actually interfered with your ability to do so?
5. If you're still having frequent episodes of overwhelming pain, anger, and grief when you're reminded of the betrayal, how are

you getting through the days? If you think about it, have you noticed some easing of the pain over time—yes, you're still hurting, but there are some times when you can feel okay? What's helped you?

Chapter 7

Are You Ready to Forgive?

How Do You Know You're Ready to Forgive?

As we discussed in Chapter 6, you might not be ready to forgive. And no one else can determine that for you.

Then how *do* you know when you're ready to forgive?

Well, first consider whether you're in one of those circumstances we discussed in Chapter 6 in which you still need the anger you've been feeling.

If you're still in an abusive situation, you're not ready to forgive. You need to get out and get safe. The anger you feel is there to help you do that.

And even when you're safe, if you're still working through the trauma you've experienced, anger is part of that process. In particular, directing your anger outward, toward whoever hurt you rather than at yourself, is an important stage in recovering from what happened.

Essentially, you're ready to forgive when you can think about the events that hurt you and recognize that you have some leeway about how you react to the memory.

In other words, you're ready to forgive when you're no longer triggered into panic by a reminder of what happened. You're ready when you can think about it calmly, with perspective and nuance.

How Do You Cope if You're Not Ready to Forgive?

Many of you reading this are not at all ready to forgive the betrayal that happened to you.

You're still reeling from it. The pain, confusion, and anger you feel when you're reminded of it are still overwhelming. And it seems automatic and unavoidable. That leeway about how you react that I mentioned above? It's just not there. You probably sought out this book because you want help feeling better, and fast.

How do you get through the day when that's happening?

I've got bad news and good news for you.

The bad news is that there's no magic formula for getting through the pain. Like any kind of grief, healing from betrayal requires what it requires. You'll have moments when things are starting to seem okay, and moments when it seems like the hurt will never stop. The best you can do is make as much room for the grief as it needs, while still doing what you need to do.

In some ways, the grief of being betrayed is similar to the grief of losing a loved one to death. You're in mourning. Yes, I understand that being betrayed isn't the same as being a mourner. You don't get the community support that comes with having lost a loved one to death. Worse, the betrayal may have cost you the one person whom you counted on the most for help when you need it.

But you can still apply the wisdom of mourning traditions to your situation.

For example, in my own Jewish tradition, when you've lost a close relative (parent, spouse, sibling, or child) there are guidelines about what's expected of you based on how long it's been since the loss. Before the funeral of your relative, essentially nothing is expected of you. During the seven days (called "shiva," meaning seven) starting with the funeral, slightly more is expected of you, but you're still freed of most regular responsibilities, and the community take cares of your needs by bringing food and religious services to your home. After that, you're expected to fulfill your usual obligations, but at a reduced level for the remainder of the first month after the death. When it's a parent you've lost, additional mourning restrictions hold for almost a year.

Whatever traditions you're familiar with, the idea that you need some time and emotional space to deal with a loss can be helpful as you grieve the betrayal. Give yourself some slack in terms of what you expect to be able to accomplish, at least at first. Reach out for help where you can.

As I said, there's no magic formula that will make you feel better right away. That's the bad news.

The good news? You *will* feel better—much better. You may not believe it now, but you will. It won't be as soon as you hope (which is immediately), but it will be way sooner than you fear (which is never). You'll heal from this.

One of the interesting phenomena about recovering from a deep place—be it depression, sadness, or grief—is that you don't consciously *feel* better for quite a while after you're in fact *doing* better. Actually noticing that you're doing better is a trailing, not leading, indicator of how you're functioning. That means you'll be acting better before you're aware of feeling better.

Curiously, one of the most dangerous times in terms of suicide is when someone starts to get better before they realize it consciously. The danger is that as someone comes out of the pit emotionally, they have more ability to imagine things being better—but they still feel that nothing has changed, so it makes their situation seem even worse by contrast.

If you're feeling suicidal, reach out for help—as I'm sure you know, you can call your local mental health crisis line (in the USA, you can call 988). You're reading this book because you know that feeling better is possible. It will get better!

As we'll discuss in Chapter 12, the antidote to despair is faith. Feel free to hop to that chapter if you'd like an infusion of faith.

How Do You Heal from the Trauma of Betrayal?

You're ready to forgive when you've healed from the trauma enough that you're no longer propelled into panic when you think of the betrayal. How do you get there?

It takes time, courage, and effort. You need to give yourself experiences of thinking about the betrayal and still feeling relatively safe. That's how your brain will learn that the *memory* of the betrayal isn't the same as the betrayal itself. That's how you'll be able to think about the betrayal without going into panic mode.

Of course, one of the ways you can get those healing experiences is by finding a therapist who knows how to help you process trauma. (We touched on this in Chapter 4, when I noted that forgiveness is directly related to healing from trauma.) In the past forty years or so, a number of therapeutic modalities have been developed that are specifically geared toward healing the effects of trauma. In my own practice I've helped people using EMDR (Eye Movement Desensitization and Reprocessing), and there are others—just look for approaches that have solid research support.[4]

And therapy isn't the only way. You might be able to process the trauma by talking with supportive friends (though beware of friends trying to tell you how to feel, as we discussed in Chapter 6). You might find that just getting on with your life has the effect of giving you those healing experiences even if you're not specifically seeking them out.

However you heal, you're ready to consider forgiving when your reaction to thinking about the betrayal is no longer automatic—that is, when you recognize that you have some choice about how you react.

Of course, it's not black-and-white. You'll have times when being reminded of the betrayal is no big deal, and times when it's acutely painful. But when you're past the panic, you can consider forgiveness.

In Chapter 8 we'll consider how to forgive when you're ready. I realize you might not be ready—but feel free to read on even if you're not ready to forgive. Knowing how you might do it will be helpful when you are ready, and learning more about forgiveness might just help you get there.

Reflections on Chapter 7

1. If you're trying to heal from an experience of betrayal, think back over the past few days. When you've thought about the betrayal, how have you reacted? Has there been some variation in your reactions? Do you notice that some moments are worse than others? What seems to make the difference?

---

[4] I wrote more about this in my book *Reigniting the Spark*.

2. Think about those moments when you've been reminded of the betrayal. When you've had a rush of strong feelings—anger, panic, grief, whatever—what seems to help you recover?

3. Can you imagine being able to think about what happened but still stay relatively calm? That would mean being able to let go of anger and blame—in other words, to forgive. Whom do you blame for what happened? Do you blame yourself partly? Do you blame reality in general? How might you let go of the blame?

Chapter 8

How Can You Forgive?

Do You Want to Forgive?

Let's check in with one of our example couples.

Greta and Van were dealing with Greta's revelation that her father had molested her when she was a child, and she hadn't told Van about it even though they had been together for decades. When they first came to see me, both of them were feeling betrayed. Van felt deeply hurt about Greta's withholding the truth about her strained relationship with her parents; to him, her lack of trust in him called their entire marriage into question. Greta felt that Van's angry reaction simply reinforced her fear that he couldn't handle the truth, and his lack of empathy for her as she tried to care for her parents felt like abandonment.

Over the course of a few sessions, they were each able to develop some perspective on their own reactions. In other words, we were able to talk about the situation without immediately triggering panic in either of them. They each still had misgivings about whether they could trust each other to be both honest and caring, but they were calmer as they thought about it.

As we discussed in Chapter 7, you're ready to forgive when you're no longer propelled into panic by reminders of the betrayal. When you realize that you have some leeway about how you react, you can use that leeway to choose forgiveness. Couples therapy, when it works well, can help you experience that leeway. That's what it did for Greta and Van.

Of course, just because you *can* choose forgiveness doesn't mean that you *want to* choose forgiveness. It's a choice. But it was clear that both Van and Greta wanted to find a way to forgive each other. For them, the choice was simple: they wanted to stay together, and didn't want to be angry and resentful anymore.

It's not surprising that Greta and Van wanted to find a way to let go of the anger—after all, they wanted to stay together. And the converse is also true: if you want to let go of the anger, which is to forgive someone, you're more likely to want to stay with them.

But, as we discussed in Chapters 4 and 5, you might want to forgive someone you have no intention of staying with. I've already talked about Flora, who forgave her violent ex-husband Jason even as she kept a gun handy in case he showed up.

And there's lots of middle ground between wanting to stay married to someone and possibly needing to shoot them if they drop by.

When I met Angie and Peter, the couple who each felt betrayed because Angie no longer wanted to work extra jobs to support Peter's unsuccessful attempts to earn money as a freelance writer, the jury was still out on whether their marriage would work out or not. But they had kids together, and had every reason to want to work together civilly or even cordially, whether or not they divorced. They weren't sure they could trust each other, but they knew they were going to be encountering each other frequently, and didn't want to be miserable every time that happened.

Sarah and Phil were also painfully uncertain about how their marriage would go, though neither wanted to split up. Sarah's discovery of Phil's cross-dressing, and the fact that he kept it secret for decades, had her questioning everything about their marriage. Phil wanted Sarah to believe that he still loved her and desired her sexually, and to understand why he kept his cross-dressing secret. They both wanted to get past the sense of betrayal.

Albert still maintained hope for their 40-year marriage, even after Beth had left and pursued a relationship with another man. When the man dumped her and she wanted to come back to Albert, he realized that he'd have to get past his anger to make that possible, and he didn't know how. But he knew he needed to find a path to forgiveness, even to be able to decide whether the marriage was viable.

Forgiveness is about your own freedom. That's the reason to want to forgive if you can. You still have to make the choice.

We're about to talk about three steps to forgiveness, but I suppose step zero is to choose to take step one.

Three Steps to Forgiveness

You've processed the trauma to the point that you can think about the betrayal without immediately freaking out. And you've recognized that letting go of the anger is the way to freedom. You want to find a way to forgive. (If you're not there yet, read on anyway.)

How do you do it? How do you forgive someone for betraying you?

It's a three-step process:

1. Forgive yourself.

2. Forgive whoever hurt you.
3. Forgive God.

Let's talk about each step.

Reflections on Chapter 8

1. Whether or not you're ready to forgive, why might you want to? Besides the general idea that letting go of anger feels good, are there particular circumstances you're dealing with that make forgiveness desirable? For example, will you be continuing to have contact with whoever betrayed you, as you would if you're co-parenting?

2. Even if you're not going to be in contact with the one who betrayed you, are there reasons you might want to forgive anyway?

3. We're about to get into the three steps to forgiveness that I outlined. Before we do, think about each one. Why might you need to forgive yourself, and why do I put that first, before you forgive whoever hurt you? And whatever might it mean to forgive God?

Chapter 9

Forgive Yourself

Self-Blame as an Adaptation

The first of the three steps to forgiveness is to forgive yourself.

Any time we're hurt, we're at least partly inclined to blame ourselves.

That's obviously true when the hurt was caused by something I did to myself, and knew better. The third time I trip on the same tree root, I have nobody but myself to blame. Watch out for the damn tree root!

It's more complicated when the hurt was interpersonal, but even then I can often see that I contributed to the situation. If someone yelled at me, it could be that they're being a bully or having a bad day or forgot to take their medications. But it might just be that I was a jerk, and they're reacting to it. At least considering the possibility that I contributed to the problem is part of basic accountability.

Those are times when blaming myself, at least to some extent, is justified. We'll come back to those times when we talk about moving on.

But what about situations where you didn't cause the hurt, didn't see it coming, and couldn't have prevented it even if you did?

Even then, we still tend to blame ourselves for letting it happen.

We've talked about Greta, who was molested by her father when she was 12 years old. Unlike many children, she was able to find a way to prevent it from happening after the third time, by avoiding her father.

But many survivors of sexual abuse were much younger when it began, or had other reasons they weren't able to prevent it from repeating again and again. I've worked with adults who were sexually abused starting at three, continuing for years. And even when it's obvious to an adult mind that a three-year-old couldn't have stopped an adult from abusing them, the survivors still tend to blame themselves for not stopping it.

There's a reason for that tendency toward self-blame even in situations where there's no rational or moral culpability.

We blame ourselves because it's better than the alternative. If a young child doesn't blame herself, she's left with a world in which she's at the mercy of malevolent forces over which she has no control—and the people she needs to be protecting her are part of those forces. At least if she blames herself, she has the illusion of some control over it. The alternative is sheer terror.

In other words, self-blame is adaptive when you have little control over what's happening. It's not an *accurate* read on the situation, but it makes it more possible to tolerate it with less panic. It's similar to simply denying that something terrible is actually happening. It helps get you through the immediate fear.

Just as denial doesn't work in the long run, self-blame doesn't work in the long run either. Blaming yourself doesn't actually prevent someone from harming you, and can make you more vulnerable to abuse since you might not recognize the red flags coming from someone else.

But it's important to recognize that self-blame is not a crazy strategy. Self-blame is an adaptation to an otherwise intolerable situation.

When you've been betrayed as an adult, part of the early phase of denial is often a feeling that you can make the betrayal go away if you just…well, if you just do *something*. In other words, it must have been your fault, somehow. If only you had been a better lover, or lost weight, or paid more attention to your partner's social media posts, or…whatever, you could have prevented the betrayal. And if you do those things now, you can reverse it.

As you probably realize already, those desperate thoughts are false. You *couldn't* prevent it.

I once worked with a woman who came to me after her husband had killed himself in such an unusual way that no one could have predicted it beforehand. He went out in the morning, ostensibly to go to the store, and never returned. The woman I worked with blamed herself for not stopping him from going out, or at least accompanying him. She was convinced she should have seen it coming, even though she acknowledged that there had been no sign of suicidality before. In particular, she blamed herself for not stopping him from doing what he did, even as she recognized that no one could have predicted it.

Self-blame is a powerful coping mechanism, even when you know it's irrational.

Then how do you forgive yourself? How can you get past blaming yourself for not preventing what happened to you?

How Do You Forgive Yourself?

To forgive yourself when you've been betrayed is to recognize that you were doing the best you could under the circumstances.

That last phrase is crucial: "under the circumstances." That includes the circumstance of what you knew and didn't know at the time. Now that you've been through the betrayal, it's easy to judge yourself harshly. But you didn't know the betrayal would happen—until it did.

Kimberly blamed herself for not realizing what Matt was up to. *I should have known he was unhappy with our sex life. Why didn't I speak up when I noticed he was coming home late all those times? Now look what's happened!*

But Kimberly *didn't* know then what she knows now. She *didn't* know what was going to happen. And neither did you.

To forgive yourself is a combination of accepting the reality of what happened, and extending compassion to the person you were before the betrayal. Yes, if you had known what was coming, you might have acted differently—but you *didn't* know what was coming. You weren't crazy, or stupid. You were just human, with limited information and understanding.

Even if you now see that you were in denial, that the truth was there for you to see but you refused to see it—well, you were just doing what most of us do. When a situation seems hopeless, sometimes the best you can do is pretend that it's not happening. Sometimes you don't see it because you cannot even conceive that someone—especially someone you love--would do that to you.

To forgive yourself is to accept that you're part of the human family, susceptible to error, misjudgment, and misinformation. You've always been part of it—now you know it even better. And just as you can feel compassion for someone else who was hurt because they didn't know enough to prevent it, you can extend that compassion to yourself.

To forgive yourself means that you accept that no matter how careful you are, sometimes you'll fail to pick up the signs that you're about to get hurt. And sometimes you'll simply make mistakes and get hurt as a result. Learn from those mistakes, yes, but you don't have to stay angry at yourself. You can even appreciate the wisdom you've gained.

That's what it means to forgive yourself.

How do you do it? You start by choosing forgiveness rather than self-blame. And that choice involves faith—which we'll talk about in Chapter 12. For now, simply know that you can have compassion for yourself for being human. You did the best you could under the circumstances, even if the best you could do wasn't so great.

Reflections on Chapter 9

1. Thinking about your own experience of betrayal, do you still blame yourself for some part of it? Even if you don't feel you did anything morally wrong, have you blamed yourself for not preventing the betrayal, or at least seeing it coming?
2. If you have blamed yourself in some way, are you still angry with yourself? Do you still find yourself trying to rewrite what happened in your mind?
3. I talked in this chapter about forgiving yourself as a recognition that you were doing the best you could *under the circumstances*. The circumstances, of course, included what you knew or didn't know, and what you were able to imagine or not. Are you able to grant yourself that understanding?
4. If you are able to understand that you were doing the best you could under the circumstances, can you extend yourself compassion for being human? As I said in the chapter, welcome

to the human family, all of us susceptible to error. Does that awareness bring you some comfort?

5. If you can recognize your commonality with the rest of us, how might that affect how you see the person who betrayed you?

Chapter 10

Forgive Whoever Hurt You

Forgiving Others: An Extension of Forgiving Yourself

The second of our three steps to forgiveness is to forgive whoever hurt you.

This is a good time to remind yourself of what forgiveness is and isn't, as we discussed in Chapter 4. Forgiveness isn't minimizing or justifying or forgetting what happened. Forgiving someone doesn't mean that you trust them—trust involves a whole different set of considerations. Forgiving someone doesn't require that they show remorse (though that will certainly bear on whether you can trust them going forward). And forgiving someone doesn't imply that you'll restore your relationship with them, or even continue it at all.

No, forgiving whoever hurt you just means you can think about them without being preoccupied by anger or panic. You're free to get on with your life. Encountering them or being reminded of them won't ruin your day.

How can you do that?

Once you've forgiven yourself, to extend that forgiveness to whoever hurt you is actually a short step.

Think again about what it means to forgive yourself. It means you accept that you were doing the best you could under the circumstances. With hindsight you can see where you went wrong, but you accept that you couldn't have known what would happen until it did. And—crucially—you extend compassion to yourself for being that normal, mistake-prone human being who failed to prevent the betrayal from happening.

To forgive whoever hurt you is pretty much the same sort of acceptance. It means that whoever hurt you was doing the best they could under the circumstances.

Doing the Best They Could

Seriously? That cheating, lying, no-good bastard who betrayed me was doing the best he could?

No—just the best he could *under the circumstances.* Because those circumstances include the sum total of what he knew, felt, believed, and was trained in at that moment. That sum probably included a slew of inaccuracies, pernicious prejudices, and self-justifying rationalizations. But that's what he was working with, along with a unique history of his own, just as you have.

I'm not trying to let him off the hook morally. He made choices, and should be held accountable for them. The devil didn't make him do it—he chose to do it himself. Remember, forgiving him doesn't absolve him of responsibility for anything.

But in doing what he did, he was being human, just as you were when you failed to protect yourself adequately. And remaining angry at him (assuming you're out of danger) is no more helpful than remaining angry at yourself. You might not trust him. You might not want to stay in any kind of active relationship with him. But you don't have to stay angry. You might even be able to understand something of what he was going through, and have some empathy.

I've mentioned Flora's ability to forgive her ex-husband Jason, who had violently assaulted her repeatedly and threatened to kill her and their children. Flora's description of how she could forgive Jason was straightforward: she no longer needed to be preoccupied with anger at someone who was basically crazy. I don't think she meant crazy in a legal sense—just in the sense that there was no point expecting him to become safe to be around, or struggle emotionally with how to deal with him. She just had to keep away from him.

Albert's path to forgiving his wife Beth, who had abruptly separated from him to pursue an affair and then wanted to come back when the affair partner ended it, was more complicated. He was clear—as was Beth—that her actions were morally wrong, at least the part about cheating on him while they were still together. But he also recognized that they had both been suppressing some longstanding problems between them, which made it harder for Beth to come to him and talk things over. He came to understand how that could have made her more vulnerable to the lure of an affair. Just as he could forgive himself for not seeing the disaster coming, he could forgive Beth for not heading it off.

Remember Ann Lamott's hilarious metaphor: not forgiving someone is like drinking rat poison and waiting for the rat to die. And as Lamott and a bunch of other writers have pointed out, forgiving means you give up hope of changing the past. Your continuing anger has been an effort by the part of your brain that doesn't know any better to make the betrayal *not have happened*—in other words, to change the past. When you forgive the one who hurt you, you stop trying to do that. You may still need to grieve, but your grieving is about what is behind you, not what lies ahead.

And when you stop trying to change the past, you can get on with figuring out how to deal with the present. In terms of the one who betrayed you, you can figure out how you want to relate to them going forward.

Forgiveness as an Inside Job

Are you surprised that I'm claiming that this step, forgiving whoever hurt you, is actually easier than forgiving yourself?

Remember back in Chapter 4 when we talked about forgiveness as an inside job? When you recognize that forgiveness isn't about the one who hurt you—it's really about yourself and your own reactions—then you can see why letting go of anger is the key skill, regardless of the object of the anger.

And if you try to do our first two steps to forgiveness in reverse order—that is, if you try to forgive whoever hurt you while you're still angry at yourself for letting it happen—it just won't work. If you're still angry at yourself, you haven't accepted the essential reality: even doing the best you can, you can still get hurt.

If you think you're forgiving someone who betrayed you by directing all the anger at yourself, you're just deluding yourself. They *did* betray you. Even if you contributed to the problem, it *wasn't* all your fault.

And even if what happened was somehow all your fault, continuing to berate yourself about it won't help you act responsibly going forward.

But you know better than that. If you really thought whoever hurt you was blameless, you wouldn't be reading a book about betrayal.

No, the hard part is forgiving yourself. When you can accept with emotional and rational clarity that you did the best you could, you can consider whether you can extend that same understanding—and compassion—to whoever hurt you.

But even when you can forgive yourself, and forgive whoever hurt you, there's another step I think is every bit as crucial to your healing.

Reflections on Chapter 10

1. A lot of people get stuck at the idea that the one who betrayed you was doing the best they could. How do you feel about that idea? When you think about your own situation, can you imagine extending that kind of forgiveness to the one who betrayed you? Or does it seem like making excuses for the inexcusable?

2. I've pointed out that you can still hold someone morally and legally responsible for what they did even if you forgive them. Can you imagine that? For example, can you imagine testifying against someone who hurt you but still not being angry? Or can you imagine divorcing someone and pursuing financial accountability while still having some understanding of why they did what they did? Why might you want that?

3. Before you start the next chapter, give some thought to what I might mean by the need to forgive God. Do this even if you don't believe in God, or find the idea of God problematic.

Chapter 11

Forgive God

What Do You Think About God?

The first two steps to forgiveness involve how you feel toward specific people involved in the betrayal: yourself, and whoever hurt you. As we've discussed in Chapters 9 and 10, you need to accept that you did the best you could under the circumstances. And when you've accepted that, it's a short step to extend that same understanding to whoever hurt you.

The third step to forgiveness is to forgive God.

Huh? Forgive God?

I'm going to assume your own attitudes about God are in one of three categories (I know this is oversimplified, but bear with me):

1. You don't believe in God—or more specifically, you're convinced that there is no God. There is no First Cause, no Unmoved Mover, and certainly no guy with a white beard up

in the sky with whom you can chat. The universe unfolds through its own unintelligent processes, not because some celestial puppeteer is pulling the strings. Prayer is delusional. "God" is an archaic concept, useful for people who don't understand how science works, or for people who can't tolerate uncertainty and want ready-made instructions on how to live. And as bad as the idea of "God" is, "religion" is even worse, responsible for much of the violence and intolerance that plagues humanity.

2. You're not fond of the idea of "God"—it seems too much like that guy with a beard I mentioned in describing category 1. But you describe yourself as spiritual. You might say you know there's more than just what we can sense—there's some kind of power beyond our understanding. You're not comfortable with religion, especially organized religion, but you're open to some of what religions talk about.

3. You do believe in God. You know, through a combination of your own experiences and your trust in the experiences of others you respect, that God is real, hears us, and cares about us. You believe we are here to do what God wants us to do, because God wants the best for us. Perhaps your beliefs are shaped by a particular religious tradition, which specifies doctrines you accept as true.

As I said, I know this is oversimplified, but when I say the third step to forgiveness is to "forgive God," your reaction is bound to be affected by which of those categories most closely describes your attitude. I feel like I'm addressing three different audiences.

Fundamentalism versus Non-fundamentalism

Wonder where I am among the three? Well, before I tell you, I need to make one more distinction, this one defining two categories:

fundamentalist or non-fundamentalist. I should note here that I'm using the term "fundamentalist" in a generic sense, not in reference to any particular group that may use the term in its name.

If you're fundamentalist, you believe that the doctrines you espouse are true and unchangeable. They aren't open to debate. Anyone who questions them is at least misinformed, and possibly deluded by evil forces. You might have compassion for such misguided people, but you're not particularly interested in how they came to their incorrect views. If you interact with them at all, you want to persuade them to accept the truth.

If you're non-fundamentalist, you also have beliefs that are important to you. But you recognize that no one has perfect knowledge and understanding of reality. When you encounter information that contradicts or challenges your views, you consider the possibility of modifying your views. People who hold other views presumably do so because their experience and frame of reference is different from yours—not because they are misguided or evil. When you encounter them, you're curious, even though you may disagree.

I've met members of very conservative religious communities who are not at all fundamentalist as I'm using the term. They are open to hearing other ideas, even as they adhere faithfully to the norms, beliefs, and practices of their own community. Fundamentalism isn't at all the same as conservatism.

And just as being religiously conservative doesn't mean being fundamentalist, being religiously non-conservative doesn't mean being non-fundamentalist. For example, I've met passionate atheists whose closed-minded attitude towards religion in general fits my definition of fundamentalism to a tee.

Now I can tell you where my own attitudes about God fall in the spectrum: pretty much everywhere *except* fundamentalist. What I'm saying in this section, I think, is relevant to anyone, whether you find the idea of God problematic, mysterious, or reassuring.

Personally, I find the idea of God all of those: problematic, mysterious, and reassuring.

But if you're fundamentalist about your own beliefs, I suspect the idea of forgiving God won't make a lot of sense, wherever you are on the spectrum of beliefs about God. In fact, I think fundamentalism makes genuine forgiveness nearly impossible, because forgiveness requires an ability to reconsider your understandings about pretty much anything.

So I'm writing this from a non-fundamentalist viewpoint.

And if you *are* fundamentalist and nevertheless want to understand what I'm saying—well, by my definition you're not as fundamentalist as you think you are. Read on.

A Note About Terminology

As you'll see in the discussion below, I am choosing to use the pronoun "he" in referring to God. For some of you that will be unremarkable—you're probably in category 3. If you're in category 1, you probably don't much care how I refer to the non-existent God. But for those of you in categories 2 and 3 who find that choice problematic, here's why I made it.

The reason a lot of people object to speaking of God in personal terms at all, never mind gender, is that it evokes human-like imagery—and God isn't human. Then when you use male pronouns, you get the aforementioned guy with a white beard. It's reinforcing the notion of God as a father-figure, thereby excluding God as a mother-figure, or just a friend.

I appreciate those objections. If you're trying to broaden the idea of God to invite anyone, especially girls and women, to recognize the divine power within them, restricting references to male pronouns is an obstacle. Hence the efforts in many texts to avoid gendering God

("Godself," for example), or to move back and forth between genders.

But there's a baby that gets thrown out with that bathwater.

Start by recognizing that *any* description of God that evokes a physical image is necessarily metaphorical. Why does the Bible refer to the "hand" of God? It's a metaphor for God's active power. And metaphors that evoke human-like imagery invite us to relate to God as we do to another person, not merely an airy philosophical concept. It's not about God's attributes; rather, it's about our own human ability to relate.

When we refer to God as gendered, of course, it's equally metaphorical. God is not literally male, female, or any other kind of gender. Yes, I know that the overwhelming imbalance in favor of the masculine in common usage leaves many women feeling second-class.

But here's the zinger. When I talk about needing to forgive God, I'm not talking about the feminine version. I'm specifically talking about that masculine image that we all think of. We don't need to forgive God the Mother. It's God the Father we need to forgive. That's who you're angry at.

What's the difference? It's the difference between the feminine and masculine aspects within everyone. (Read what people who are into tantra say about this—one of my favorites is a book by Katrina Bos called *Tantric Intimacy*.) The masculine is the side that plans, initiates, and executes. The feminine is the side that inspires, listens, and receives. The masculine is logic, the feminine is intuition. The masculine is structure, the feminine is flow.

Notice that this whole feminine/masculine distinction isn't really about God; it's about how we think of God at different times. In other words, it's about the particular metaphors that touch our hearts.

And in this case, I'm saying we need the masculine one.

The God we need to forgive is the one who put together a universe in which disasters like betrayal happen. Not the God who comforts and nurtures. The God who makes the rules and enforces them. Him.

Don't We Need God to Forgive Us?

Let's review the first two steps to forgiveness. Forgiving yourself means that you accept that you were doing the best you could do under the circumstances. As we discussed, that's usually the hard part. Extending that forgiveness to whoever hurt you is a (relatively) short step once you've forgiven yourself.

If you feel a personal relationship with God—that's you, category 3 people—then forgiving yourself entails recognizing that he forgives you. The big three monotheistic religions, Judaism, Christianity, and Islam, all provide ways to access God's forgiveness. When you're genuinely contrite for your own part in what happened, and do what you can to clean up the mess, then God forgives you. Then, when you genuinely accept your own inability to prevent the betrayal, you can forgive yourself.

I've known quite a few people who were convinced that they were betrayed by a loved one as punishment by God for some perceived misdeed. They couldn't forgive themselves as long as they believed that God didn't forgive them; they just felt they deserved what happened. They were stuck at step 1.

I don't know a way past that except to develop a different understanding of God. For people in some fundamentalist groups, that's tantamount to heresy, and might get them ostracized. Their choice is either to blame themselves for whatever happens to them, thereby tolerating abuse, or to lose their family, friends, and community.

But most of you reading this book aren't dealing with that choice. Whatever your relationship to God, you're able to see that God can forgive you.

No, the challenge for most of us isn't whether God can forgive us. It's whether we can forgive God.

Why Do We Need to Forgive God?

Why do we need to forgive God? For the same reason we need to forgive whoever else hurt us: so we can be free of the anger and get on with our lives.

I said we need to forgive "whoever *else* hurt us," because when you've been betrayed, it's not only a person who betrayed you. God betrayed you too.

Does that sound like blasphemy, category 3 people? Well, I come from a tradition of holding God to account. In Genesis 18, God is threatening to destroy everyone in Sodom. Abraham points out that there might be some righteous people there, and says to him, "Should not the judge of all the earth do justice?" In Exodus 35, Moses speaks up when God threatens to wipe out the people for their sin in worshipping a golden calf, and reminds him of his promises that they will thrive—essentially, Moses says to him, "Hey, this was your idea, and you promised it would work out. Get hold of yourself and stop with the destruction talk."

Isn't God supposed to be a loving father? Isn't he supposed to be all-powerful? How could he let us be betrayed? Couldn't he have intervened? Even if he wouldn't step in to change the betrayer's mind (that pesky "free will" problem), couldn't he at least have prepared us?

This failure of God to protect us from betrayal is itself a betrayal. We expect God, just like a father, to be there for us, not to desert us right when we need him. Even if your own father didn't live up to that expectation, you expect God to do better.

Even if you're in category 1—a committed atheist—I think you feel something like anger at God when you're betrayed. Why does life have to have such pain in it? We didn't deserve this. Why did the universe let this happen? Why haven't we evolved ways of avoiding this shock and despair? Where's the justice?

How Do You Forgive God?

As we've discussed, the way we forgive ourselves, and forgive whoever hurt us—steps 1 and 2—is to accept that we all did the best we could under the circumstances.

But it's hard to extend that same forgiveness to God. After all, he created the circumstances. (Or if you're in category 1 or 2, you might say he *is* the circumstances.) We can think of people as misinformed or misguided or simply error-prone. But how could God have failed to know what would happen, or if he knew, how could he be so cruel as to let it happen? What was he thinking?

And, like Job in the Bible, we're not going to let him off the hook by blaming ourselves. We dealt with that at step 1. As Job pointed out, sorry, God, I know I'm imperfect, but I didn't deserve this.

If I'm going to forgive God, I'm going to have to accept that he had his own good reasons for not intervening. And I'm also going to have to accept that I can't fully understand those reasons.

To let go of my anger at God for letting me be betrayed—in other words, to forgive God—I need to accept that this whole existence business is essentially right to be what it is. Even when it hurts.

That attitude, that reality is right to be what it is, is what I call faith.

What if you can't accept the rightness of reality? How can you find that sort of faith? Those are the topics of Chapter 12.

Reflections on Chapter 11

1. Think about my three categories of people with respect to how you understand the idea of God. Do you fit in any of the categories, or maybe in some combination? When you hear "God" what comes to mind?

2. Can you accept that life can still be worth living even though betrayals can happen? That you can heal and experience joy again, even though you've suffered? How do those possibilities fit with the idea of forgiving God?

3. We're about to get into a discussion of faith, which I define as accepting that reality is right to be what it is. What comes to your mind when you hear the word "faith?" How do your associations with the idea of faith overlap with the idea of accepting reality as right? How do your associations differ from that idea?

Chapter 12

What is Faith?

Why Faith?

A few years into my private practice, a colleague and I were on our way out of a consultation group meeting when he said to me, "How do you do couples therapy, anyway?"

That question got me thinking.[5] Of course, both my colleague and I knew it was a silly question, asking for a "standing on one foot" explanation of a complex topic. We'd each done trainings describing all sorts of ways of understanding and practicing couples therapy. But a question like that can help pare away the jargon and get to what

---

[5] And if you've read my previous books, tuned into the "Couples Therapy in Seven Words" podcast my wife Judy Alexander and I do, or watched my videos on YouTube, you've heard about it before.

really matters. How *did* I do couples therapy? What guided me, and what was I offering the couples who consulted me?

I said something like, "When I boil it down, I suppose I'm telling people, 'Be kind and don't panic.'"

Which is to say, if you can manage to avoid panic, maybe you can be kind.

Most of the techniques I had learned in training were about helping people deal with their situation without freaking out. At least if they're not in a panic, they have some chance to be decent to each other. And if they're being decent, they can figure out what they want to do. Hence, don't panic, so you can be kind.

I found that five-word formula—"Be kind and don't panic"—to be a nice way of summarizing what I did. When I described it to couples I was working with, they often found it helpful too. The idea that panic seriously interferes with kindness, and therefore messes up their relationship, fit with their experience. They could see that one of the keys to moving forward was to avoid panic, even when the situation was scary.

But then they would say, "Okay. Then how can we not panic?"

I didn't have much of an answer at first. It seemed like anything I could come up with was essentially reiterating the concept of "don't panic," except with more syllables.

Even though I didn't have an immediate answer, as I thought about the people I worked with, I did notice that some of them seemed to do better than others in the "don't panic" department. If I could understand what contributed to that ability, maybe I'd have something to offer when people asked how they could avoid panic.

I could tell that the difference wasn't about how difficult their situation was; there were folks who completely freaked out over what seemed even to them to be pretty trivial difficulties, and folks who seemed to stay relatively calm even in very dire situations. And it didn't seem to depend on which clever techniques I was teaching them.

What was it about those people who could actually manage the five-word formula, especially the "don't panic" part? What did they have that the others didn't?

Well, if you asked the Cowardly Lion that question, he'd say, "Courage!" But I like a different word: faith.

What I noticed is that the people who were good at avoiding panic came to the work with a particular mindset, which I call faith.

Faith in Practice

Elsie and Charles were the couple who came to me after Elsie found out she had contracted herpes from Charles, which led to his admitting to hiring prostitutes for years. By the time of our first meeting, Elsie had reined in her anger at Charles enough to be able to have a session together with him. But she had no interest in understanding his experience, or even healing from her own anger. Any exploration of how Charles made the choices he made was simply offering him excuses. Forgiveness was out of the question. She only wanted to stay together because she couldn't imagine giving up the lifestyle they had, and couldn't bear the humiliation if their friends and family found out what Charles had done. As Elsie described it, she wanted to see Charles suffer the way she had. Charles, for his part, just wanted to get past it all somehow, and saw Elsie's desire to punish him as simply what he deserved.

Greta and Van were also in a lot of pain when they first consulted me. They each felt betrayed—Van, because Greta hadn't trusted him enough to tell him about her experiences of molestation by her father, and Greta, because Van's anger at her for keeping the secret, and for her continued relationship with her parents, felt like abandonment.

But Greta and Van approached the work very differently from how Elsie and Charles did. Even though both Greta and Van were hurt and angry about each other's reactions, they knew they needed to try to understand those reactions, rather than simply reject them.

To put it another way, each of them came to the work already knowing that whatever the other had done had some basis for it. Neither one of them was crazy, nor evil. Scared, maybe. Unsure, maybe. Not fully aware of all the facts, maybe. But not crazy or evil. Whatever happened, however painful, must have some rightness to it under the circumstances. If they could understand that, maybe they could appreciate the difficult choices they each made, even if they wished they had made different choices.

The people I worked with who showed that mindset—that whatever happened must have some rightness to it, even if they can't fully understand it—are the people who could face their situations without panic. They accepted that reality was right to be what it was, and worked with it rather than railed against it. That mindset was what made the difference.

Why Call It "Faith"?

I chose to call that mindset—that reality is right to be what it is—"faith." Now I had an answer to the question, "How do you not panic?" Since faith lets you not panic, the five-word formula became a seven-word formula: "Be kind, don't panic, and have faith." If you learn the mindset of faith—and I came to see that's it's a learnable mindset—then you can handle what happens without panic.

I realize that using the word "faith" invites some confusion with other ways of using the word.

Sometimes people use the word "faith" to mean certainty about the truth of something. The quintessential example of faith-as-certainty is in the expression, "I have faith in God," usually meaning, "I believe that God exists," often with the implication, "I believe that

God will take care of me." In that sense, having faith means that, even though you don't know exactly how, somehow things will work out okay.

After all, God has a plan. So shut up and accept it.

That's *not* what I mean by "faith." I don't pretend to know that things will work out okay, whatever that might mean. And I don't think you should just shut up and accept it. If it's somehow all in God's plan, I think being angry at God for causing you all that pain is entirely justifiable. In fact, as we discussed when we talked about forgiveness, I think anger is a necessary part of healing from betrayal. That's why forgiving God is a necessary step—if you weren't angry at him, you wouldn't have to forgive him.

No, what I mean by "faith" isn't about what you believe.

Nor is faith about any degree of certainty. One of the realities we need to accept is that we have limited information and limited ability to understand it. Certainty is an illusion. That's why fundamentalism is not based on faith at all. To claim that you know *anything* for certain is the opposite of faith, because it refuses to accept the reality that humans aren't God, with an omniscient view of the universe.

Rather, faith is a mindset, an orientation to life. When you're manifesting faith, you act in ways that reflect a view that life is right to be what it is, even when it's difficult. Since reality is right to be what it is, you're right to be who you are. So you use the power you have to do the best you can.

I'm neither theologian nor philosopher—and, meaning no disrespect to those professions, I'm very happy with that fact. But those of you who are so inclined might want to check out Martin Buber's distinction between the Hebrew word *emunah* and the Greek word *pistis*, both often translated as "faith." Essentially, *pistis* refers to faith as belief in some proposition—in other words, *pistis* is about what you know or believe to be true. But *emunah* refers to faith as a way of acting, not a way of believing. *Emunah* is not about what you believe. It's about how your actions reveal what you trust. You might not have any particular beliefs about God or existence in general that you can articulate, but if you act in a way that reflects trust that this whole existence business is somehow good, you're acting with *emunah*.

Not surprisingly, I've gone with the Hebrew concept rather than the Greek one. The faith I'm talking about isn't about what you believe; it's about how you act.

This means that faith isn't "true" or "false." *Facts* are true or false. Science is about facts, and if science challenges my long-held beliefs, I'd better question my long-held beliefs. (By the way, even science—at least, good science—isn't *certain* about facts; scientists are just trying to explain the data they have as well as they can. That's why scientists are eager to test and question their own theories in light of new data.)

But faith isn't about what's true or false. Rather, faith is about how I act in the face of the facts, whatever they are. To act with faith is to treat reality—including your own part in it—as basically good, worth the effort of participating. A person of faith isn't at all certain about what the facts *are*. But they are willing to deal with *whatever* the facts are, because the whole game is worth playing.

I'm guessing you know people who reflect this mindset of faith. They're the ones who face illness, natural disasters, and, yes, betrayal with a determination to do what they can, rather than giving up in despair. They're the ones who keep living until they die, and face even the certainty of death with courage. And when you're with them, you sense acceptance, compassion, and respect—because they see you, and themselves, as essentially valid, screw-ups and all.

How Do You Acquire Faith?

As a client of mine once put it, "Wow—faith sounds like the stuff to have. Where can I get me some?"

Well, that's like asking where you can get Rafa's backhand or Simone's vault or Tiger's drive. You could read about Rafa's backhand or Simone's vault or Tiger's drive. You could learn to describe what they do, and get an idea of the physiological principles involved.

But if you want to *do* it like they do, you'll have to practice.

Faith isn't a set of knowledges or beliefs. If it were, you could bone up on it the way you study for a history test. But it's not. Faith is a skill.

Faith is about how you act, not about what you know or believe. And even though I can try to convince you that practicing faith has benefits—that, after all, is the main point of this chapter—I can't convince you that faith is a more *correct* or *accurate* guideline for behavior, because it isn't. You can find all sorts of evidence that reality is beautiful and worth participating in, and all sorts of evidence that reality is horrible and pointless. Which evidence you'll tend to see is based on your mindset. Neither view is more correct than the other—these aren't statements of fact, they're value judgments.

Like any other skill, you acquire faith by practicing it. And, like any other skill, practicing faith is a choice.

You begin by taking the risk of opening yourself to different ideas about how life works. If you're in a spiral of despair, practicing faith means that you allow for the possibility that what you do matters, even when things feel bleak. If you're cynical about yourself and everyone else, practicing faith means questioning your cynicism. If you're convinced that you deserve to suffer, practicing faith means that you allow for the possibility that you also deserve to feel better.

Of course, to learn a skill it helps to have good teachers.

A Caveat About Religious Faith

If you're looking for teachers to help you practice faith, doesn't it make sense to turn to the "faith-based" community?

Well, this is where the different meanings of the word "faith" can lead you astray.

I've talked about the distinction between fundamentalist and non-fundamentalist understandings. In Chapter 11 my focus was on understandings of God, but the distinction can apply to pretty much any set of ideas. Fundamentalists are convinced that their ideas are true, and that contrary or alternative ideas are false. Non-fundamentalists have ideas they like, but are open to the possibility that contrary or alternative ideas have value as well.

The faith I've been describing in this chapter is non-fundamentalist. In fact, the faith I've been describing is incompatible with fundamentalism. A fundamentalist view of the world claims certainty, which denies the reality that no human can have a complete and perfect understanding of how things are.

From my own Jewish perspective (and here I don't claim to be speaking for all Jews or any particular branch of Judaism), fundamentalism is idolatry. For people to claim certainty is to set up human constructions as God, and then worship them. (As I said, I'm not speaking for all Jews, but this idea of fundamentalism as idolatry is heavily influenced by my Jewish background. And this is not just a Jewish view—Pope Francis agrees with me. Google it!)

However, I don't mean to dismiss religious traditions and religious teachers as sources of guidance to help you learn the skill of faith. On the contrary, your own religious tradition can be a great place to start, because you already speak its language.

The caveat is that a lot of people talk about a "faith-based" approach when what they mean is a fundamentalist approach. If you go to your clergyperson for help dealing with hard issues—such as a betrayal—you might get just what you need to help you on a path of faith. Or you might get closed-minded dogma. The pastors I mentioned in Chapter 6 who told women to go back and submit to their abusive husbands are egregious examples of the latter.

Of course, the same risk is true if you go to a therapist, whether they call themselves "faith-based" or not. Some therapists will exemplify faith themselves in how they work with you, which means you'll experience a sense of acceptance as well as a willingness to talk about really hard stuff without shying away from it. But some therapists will fall back on their favorite theories and diagnose you rather than listen to you—which is just another form of fundamentalism. And this tendency to force you into an ideological box rather than actually listen to you isn't restricted to "faith-based" or politically conservative practitioners. I've heard a lot of dogma from people across the political spectrum.

Unfortunately, there's no simple way to know in advance whether your clergyperson or therapist embodies faith (as I've described it) or not. And, of course, it's not an all-or-nothing characteristic. You can learn from anyone. Just be on the lookout for fundamentalism, because it won't help you develop faith.[6]

Faith and Forgiveness

We got into this discussion of faith because, I've claimed, in order to forgive a betrayal you need all three steps: forgive yourself, forgive whoever hurt you, and forgive God.

And, while you might be able to forgive yourself and forgive whoever hurt you without necessarily having a mindset of faith, I don't see how you can forgive God without faith. If I operate from a perspective that reality basically sucks, then I'm not going to be

---

[6] I wrote more about the problem of how to find a therapist who embodies faith in my book *It's Not About Communication!*

willing to cut God any slack for betraying me. It's only by adopting a perspective of faith—that reality, for all its incomprehensible and often painful weirdness, is basically good—that I can let go of my anger at God and get on with living. In fact, you could argue that "forgiving God" and "having faith" as I define it are essentially synonymous.

But I think faith is key for all three steps to forgiveness, not just for forgiving God.

How did Flora manage to forgive herself for not stopping her husband's violence before she did? How did Greta forgive herself for not doing more to protect herself as a child? How can you forgive yourself for not preventing the betrayal you've experienced?

To forgive yourself, as we said in Chapter 9, is to realize that you were doing the best you could under the circumstances. Another way to describe that realization is that you accept your own essential validity as a person. You're right to be who you are, even—especially—when you don't have enough information or insight to protect yourself from being hurt. That's the human condition. And it's right to be that way.

That's a statement of faith. Reality is right to be what it is, and you're part of that reality. Forgiving yourself is a manifestation of that faith.

And, as we said in Chapter 10, extending that forgiveness to whoever hurt you is based on the same realization. Whoever hurt you is part of that reality too, and they're right to be who they are even when they screw up royally. Forgiving whoever hurt you is also a manifestation of faith.

The third step, forgiving God, is the quintessential expression of faith. To forgive God is to recognize that existence itself is somehow right to be what it is.

To forgive is to practice faith. To practice faith is to facilitate forgiveness.

What Now?

If reading this book up to now has led you to the point that you're ready to forgive—well, *mazel tov*. (That's the Yiddish idiom for "Congratulations!") But I'm not so naïve as to think a read through this book will get you there right away. I'm guessing you're still feeling a lot of pain and confusion and anger.

Read on anyway. We're going to talk about how you can move on, once you have been able (mostly) to forgive what happened. As you'll see, forgiveness doesn't solve all your problems. But forgiveness does make it a lot easier to figure out how to handle them.

Reflections on Chapter 12

1. Now that you've read the chapter, how do you understand the idea of faith? How does faith as I described it fit in with your own experience? Even if you wouldn't have used the same term, do you feel you approach life with a mindset of faith, at least some of the time?
2. Whether or not you're skilled at practicing faith, how would a mindset of faith affect how you're recovering from betrayal?
3. I mentioned in the chapter that you can find evidence that life is beautiful and evidence that life is horrible, and that which one you're inclined to see depends on your mindset. Have you noticed this phenomenon as you've been dealing with betrayal? Are there times when everything seems bleak and hopeless, and times when you see some hope that life can be full again?
4. What might moving on mean in your situation? How will you decide?

Chapter 13

Moving On from Betrayal

What's Moving On?

Once you've been able to let go of the anger at yourself for not preventing the betrayal, and let go of the anger at whoever betrayed you, and let go of the anger at God or the universe or whatever you call your anger at reality itself—in other words, once you've accomplished the three steps of forgiveness—you're ready to move on.

As I noted at the end of the previous chapter, I realize you might not be all the way there yet. But keep reading, because thinking about moving on can help you along the path to forgiveness. Just realizing that moving on is possible can relieve some of your anxiety.

What does it mean to move on from a betrayal?

Well, it could mean a lot of different things.

Let's start by assuming you've made it past the initial shock, and you've even been able to (mostly) forgive in all the senses we've talked about. You're no longer waylaid by anger or grief when you think about what happened or are in contact with whoever hurt you. There's still pain, but there's also some clarity. You're not going to forget what happened, but you're not obsessed with it either.

In deciding how to proceed, the one choice you don't have is to move on as if nothing had happened. You can try to delude yourself and pretend otherwise, but the experience of betrayal has changed you. In particular, it's changed your relationship with the person who betrayed you. Pretending otherwise just ignores reality.

Of course, as you decide how to move on, the big question is *how* the experience has changed your relationship with the person who betrayed you. Do you want to end or recast the relationship entirely (for example, by divorcing, or curtailing contact with someone)? Or can you restore trust and heal the relationship (for example, by staying married, or continuing to have contact), perhaps even making the relationship better than it was?

Let's look at some of the possibilities.

Ending the Relationship, or Trying to Heal It?

We've mentioned Flora a few times—recall that she maintains a restraining order on her ex-husband Jason who had been violent towards her and their children. For Flora, moving on from her marriage was simple, albeit still painful. She was clear that she couldn't trust Jason, whom she still considered dangerous. She had no intention of ever seeing him or being in direct contact with him again.

But Flora also decided that she wanted to maintain contact with Jason's mother, with whom she and her children had a warm relationship. To do this, she had to trust that Jason's mother acknowledged the danger that Jason posed to her, and wouldn't reveal her whereabouts to him. Fortunately, Jason's mother was entirely cooperative, especially since she also feared Jason's potential for violence.

Moving on for Flora meant that she could concentrate on rebuilding her life. She didn't have to struggle with her decision to divorce, or worry about how to co-parent with Jason. Her decision to maintain the relationship with her ex-mother-in-law was based on a careful weighing of the risks. And her ability to do that careful weighing was facilitated by her forgiving Jason. She wasn't sidetracked by panic when she thought of him.

Flora is a great example of how you can move on when you're not stuck in anger. But Flora's situation was, in some ways, simpler than most, because she didn't have to struggle with uncertainty about how to handle the marriage. Yes, what happened to her was horrible, but at least it was clear what she needed to do.

Most of the couples I've worked with don't have that (dubious) advantage of clarity. Yes, you've been betrayed. But if the person who betrayed you isn't directly threatening your safety, you might consider trying to heal the relationship. How do you decide?

Of course, this decision depends on what kind of relationship you're dealing with. As we discussed in Chapter 3, your expectations of a spouse or committed partner are different from your expectations of a parent, adult child, or friend. Your willingness to try to heal a relationship will be based on those same expectations—and in particular, whether you can regain trust that those expectations will be met going forward.

Moreover, your willingness to try to heal a relationship will also depend on how important that relationship is to you. Deciding to terminate a friendship can be painful, but is usually much less of a disruption than terminating a marriage, or deciding to cut off contact with a family member.

Do You Have the Option of Leaving the Relationship?

We're talking in this chapter about moving on, and I've noted that you'll need to decide whether to end the relationship with the person who betrayed you, or try to heal it.

But I don't want to ignore the possibility that you might not have the luxury of making that choice.

Sarah was the woman who came home early to find her husband Phil dressed in women's clothing. They came to see me after Sarah had managed to get Phil to disclose, after some denials, that he had been cross-dressing in secret since he was a teenager, well before they married over 30 years ago.

Sarah didn't know what to make of Phil's desire to wear women's clothing. Was he gay? Was he cheating on her with men? He assured her that he's not gay, that he desired women in general and her in particular, and that hadn't cheated on her with anyone, male or female. But she didn't know if she could believe his assurances. And besides that, she didn't know how she could tolerate the idea of being married to a man who wanted to dress as a woman, even if he's not gay. It was a complete turnoff to her.

Phil tried to get Sarah to understand why he kept his cross-dressing secret from her. He had always felt conflicted about it, but had come to realize it's part of who he is. He expressed some relief that Sarah now knew about it. But he was terrified that Sarah might decide to end the marriage.

For Sarah, the prospect of ending the marriage was unthinkable. She couldn't imagine how she could survive financially—Phil had always been the one earning the money, while Sarah took care of the kids and house. She had no external employment experience. They didn't have much saved. And even with the kids grown and gone, she didn't see how they could support two households on what Phil earned—assuming she could trust Phil to continue to support her. She felt completely vulnerable.

In short, Sarah didn't feel she had the option of splitting up.

I've worked with lots of people who feel they don't have the option of splitting up for other reasons besides finances. Sometimes splitting up would mean the loss of their entire family and support structure—for example, people in religious communities that not only prohibit divorce, but ostracize anyone who defies that prohibition by going outside the community. Sometimes the prospect of splitting up feels so humiliating that a person would rather stay in a marriage with someone they don't trust.

If you feel that you don't have the option of splitting up, your prospects for how to move on are, obviously, a lot more limited. When I've worked with people who feel that way, part of the work is to explore that feeling. Are your fears realistic? Are there possibilities you haven't considered that would make the option of splitting up available?

In inviting you to consider other possibilities, I'm *not* trying to encourage you to split up (or not split up, for that matter). But, ironically, if you at least have the option to end a relationship, you have a much better chance of saving it and being happy about it, because you'll be able to give healing the relationship a try without feeling that you're consigning yourself to permanent misery if your efforts fail.

If you are clear that ending the relationship isn't an option, you can still find ways to move on from a betrayal. Spoiler alert: as we'll see, a mindset of faith is the key to moving on.

Can You Rebuild Trust?

Essentially, your decision about whether to terminate a relationship or try to heal it comes down to trust. You've been betrayed. Can you find a way to trust that the person who betrayed you won't do that again? If so, maybe you can heal the relationship.

Notice that this question is not the same as the question of forgiveness. As we've noted, you can forgive someone, in the sense of letting go of anger, but still not trust them at all.

If you haven't forgiven someone, it's very difficult to decide if you can trust them or not, because your anger gets in the way of thinking clearly about whether trust is warranted. I've met lots of people who are so distracted by their anger at someone that they aren't able to recognize that they *shouldn't* trust them. If you're internally railing at how you've been treated—in other words, you haven't forgiven—then you're still trying to change the past. Ironically, this can blind you to the possibility that you're tolerating continued mistreatment by getting angry at it instead of getting out of it.

Trust and Expectations

Let's revisit how I described betrayal back in Chapter 2. If someone betrayed you, it means they failed, in an important way, to live up to what you expect of them based on your relationship with them.

As I pointed out then, betrayal is about your expectations. Well, then so is trust. If you want to be able to trust someone after they've betrayed you, you'll need to decide if you can believe they'll live up to those expectations going forward.

In Chapter 3 I invited you to think about those expectations you have. Maybe your expectations are unrealistic, or maybe you can reconsider what you think of as important. Maybe, in other words, you don't have to think of what happened as a betrayal, but rather as a misunderstanding or a difference of values. If you can—as Patricia did, when she was able to see Zach's use of porn as something other than cheating—then the question of trust changes also. When Patricia and Zach were able to talk about their sex life more openly, Patricia no longer worried that Zach would betray her by using porn, because using porn wasn't betraying her in the first place. They could still differ on whether they approve of it, but it was no longer a matter of trust.

But I'm guessing you're reading this because you still consider what happened to you to have been a betrayal. Someone cheated on you, and you're not willing to redefine cheating to allow for what they did. Or someone double-crossed you financially, or lied about you to others, or violated your confidence, or did any of the host of other things that constitute betrayal. And no amount of re-examining your expectations has changed your view that it was indeed a betrayal.

That, after all, is why you had to go through all those steps to forgive.

Which means that you need to consider whether you can trust whoever hurt you going forward, to have any hope of healing your relationship with them.

How can you determine whether you can trust someone who has betrayed you? What are the signs?

As we noted, your willingness to try to heal a relationship will differ depending on what kind of relationship we're talking about. Deciding whether you can rebuild trust with a spouse is not the same as deciding whether you can rebuild trust with a parent or sibling or adult child or friend.

In the next two chapters we'll look at some possibilities.

Reflections on Chapter 13

1. Think about your experience of betrayal—presumably, the experience that led you to seek out this book. If the betrayal was by a spouse or committed partner, do you have the option to split up? I'm not asking if you *should* split up, or even if you want to. I'm just asking if you see splitting up as an available option. You

can ask yourself a similar question if the betrayal was from someone else—a parent, adult child, sibling, close friend, or whoever. Is ending the relationship a viable option? What would that mean in practical terms?

2. If ending the relationship is at least possible—in other words, if you see that as an option—what would you need to happen for you to choose to stay in the relationship? And even if leaving isn't an option, what would you need to happen for you to move on from the betrayal? You'd need to develop some trust that you wouldn't be betrayed again, but just what that entails might not be entirely clear. How will you know you're feeling trust again? What do you think?

3. How might you rebuild trust in your relationship with the person who betrayed you? In particular, what will you need to see/hear from them to convince you that they're trustworthy? Again, this might not be entirely clear, but give it some thought.

Chapter 14

Rebuilding Trust with a Partner

Forgiveness and Trust

If the betrayal you experienced was from a spouse or committed partner, what will it take for you to want to stay with them?

Let's say you've been able to forgive your partner, in the sense that you're no longer preoccupied with anger about the betrayal. (As before, if you're not there yet, read on anyway.) But forgiving them doesn't necessarily mean you'll want to stay with them. Recall that you can forgive someone even if you have no intention of staying with them.

If you're going to stay partnered with someone, forgiving them isn't enough. You're going to want to be able to trust them. At the least, you'll want to trust that they won't betray you again.

Yes, you can stay married or partnered with someone without trusting them. As we discussed above, I've met quite a few people who don't feel they have the option of splitting up, so they're going to stay in the relationship whether they can rebuild trust or not. And even if you do have the option, I've known people who have chosen to stay married to someone whom they no longer trust, rather than go through the pain and dislocation of separating.

But you're reading this book because you want to feel better than that.

How can you rebuild trust when your partner has betrayed you?

Do You Want to Rebuild Trust?

Of course, before you decide *how* you might rebuild trust with your partner, you'll need to consider whether you even want to rebuild trust.

Remember Kimberly and Matt? Matt had moved out, had a brief sexual relationship with a coworker, and then broke off that relationship. Kimberly accepted Matt's explanation that he had thought they were headed for divorce, but that he had realized he still loved Kimberly and wanted to stay in the marriage. She let him move back in with her on the condition that they do couples therapy. She hoped that the work they were doing in couples therapy would help them rebuild trust. And for a couple of months it seemed to be working.

Then Kimberly found out that Matt had been cheating on her with a customer much of the time they were doing couples therapy. Once she got past the initial shock and anger, she was able to think about what she wanted. She still loved Matt, and wanted to find a way to save their marriage; they had kids and a life together she didn't want to lose. But she knew she wouldn't stay in the marriage unless she could find a way to trust Matt.

And, for obvious reasons, she couldn't see how that was possible. She was willing to try, which is why she and Matt returned to couples therapy. But Kimberly realized that at this point, rebuilding trust wasn't just about finding a way to believe that Matt would be honest with her. It was also about finding a way to believe her own perceptions, and trust her own judgment. She had been badly burned. Even if she believed that Matt was sincere about wanting to understand and change his own behavior, how could she trust her own ability to judge his sincerity?

I've worked with a lot of people in Kimberly's situation. Sometimes they're able to find a way to rebuild trust, even when it seems impossible at first.

But sometimes, they decide that they don't want to try to rebuild trust. Even if they could somehow come to understand what happened, and even if they could believe that the circumstances that led to the betrayal were no longer present, and even if they could believe that their partner had learned what they needed to learn so that they would never do what they did again, and even if they have let go of anger at themselves, their partner, and God—even with all that, they recognize that there's one thing that can't be fixed: they can't make the betrayal not have happened.

And for many people, even though they've forgiven the betrayal, they won't stay with someone who betrayed them. It's not about trust going forward. Rather, it's about deciding that they can't accept having a partner who would *ever* betray them the way they did. *I may not be angry at you anymore, and I may even accept you're a good person and believe you wouldn't stray again. But I need to be with someone who hasn't strayed. I can't look at you with the same kind of respect anymore. You can't fix that.*

You'll need to decide if rebuilding trust is something you want to take on. It's not an easy decision. If you do want to rebuild trust, you'll need to accept that you are with a partner who *has* betrayed you. If you can't accept that, you're better off splitting up.

If that sounds dismal, let me offer some reassurance. The couples who *are* able to rebuild trust, and *are* able to accept that they've been through betrayal, are the couples who come to be grateful for the growth the crisis has forced on them. That doesn't always happen. But when it does, it's inspiring.

If you do want to rebuild trust with your partner, how can you do it?

What Rebuilds Trust for a Couple?

Let's first rule out some things that *don't* rebuild trust.

Becoming your partner's parole officer doesn't build trust. You can check their iPhone all you like, and it won't help you trust your partner. Of course, you could find evidence of continued cheating, which would confirm your suspicions. But if you don't find evidence of continued cheating, how many times will you need to check before you've decided you can trust your partner? You already know that if they want to evade your checking they can find a way to do so. No amount of checking will ever offer sufficient reassurance.

No, the surveillance approach simply manifests and reinforces your existing distrust. It doesn't do anything to build trust going forward.

Asking for constant reassurance from your partner doesn't work either. Their protestations that you have nothing to worry about won't convince you. They probably said similar things when they were cheating on you. And the more you ask for it, the more their reassurances ring hollow—precisely because you're asking for it so much.

Setting up rigid rules (for example, no texting after 8:00pm, no going out to a bar unless you go together, no social media) is another useless exercise if what you're trying to do is restore trust. No matter what rules you get your partner to agree to, you know they can violate them if they choose to. The rules don't protect you. And if you can actually trust your partner, you don't need rules.

Then what *does* build trust?

We said that forgiveness is an inside job—you can forgive someone without their doing anything to deserve it. But, not surprisingly, rebuilding trust in a couple involves both of you.

Building Trust Involves Both of You

To risk trusting someone who has betrayed you in the past, you'll need to find some way of understanding what they did. I don't mean *condoning* what they did. But you'll need to develop some idea of how it happened, in the sense that you can imagine how someone in the situation they were in could have made the choices they made—without being crazy or evil.

Notice how this is similar to the idea of forgiveness. You were able to forgive the person who hurt you when you could accept that they were doing the best they could *under the circumstances*. Those circumstances included how they felt, what they knew and didn't know, and anything else that was happening.

As we've noted, building trust is more than just forgiveness. Forgiveness involves accepting that your partner was doing the best they could under the circumstances. But to build trust you're going to need to feel that *the circumstances are now different*. Different enough that you can see that the betrayal wouldn't happen again. You'll need to see evidence of that.

In addition, you'll need to see evidence that your partner has a thorough understanding of what they did, what effects it had, and how the circumstances led up to the betrayal. If they didn't realize before that what they did was a betrayal, you'll need to know that they're clear about that now. If they hadn't recognized the signs that they were vulnerable to betraying you—for example, if they hadn't let themselves know they were dissatisfied with their relationship with you, or were angry with you—then you'll need to know that they've learned from the experience of betraying you, just as you've learned from the experience of being betrayed, and would bring issues up with you rather than betray you again.

Your Partner Needs to Trust You Too

Of course, part of what you'll need to experience is continued fidelity from your partner. Your alertness to the possibility that they might betray you again is an unavoidable side-effect of the betrayal. It will moderate over time, as long as your partner stays faithful, and as long as you're able to process the trauma as we discussed in Chapter 7.

But your partner's good behavior, as important as it is, isn't sufficient. To build trust, you need to know that your partner trusts you too. And you're going to have to earn that trust, just as they have to earn yours.

What? You're the one who was betrayed by your partner! Why do you need to earn your partner's trust?

Well, you betrayed them too.

Think about it. When you found out what your partner did in betraying you, what was your reaction? You were probably furious, sick, confused, and irrational—all natural responses to being betrayed. And chances are you emotionally abandoned your partner, at least some of the time. Your behavior toward them was probably more than a little harsh on numerous occasions.

Yes, I know they had it coming! This isn't about justice. I'm just saying that if you're trying to rebuild trust, you'll need to understand that your partner has had reason to doubt your love too, just as you have had reason to doubt theirs. You'll need your partner to develop an understanding of your actions, and possibly forgive you too.

In fact, you might even have to consider the possibility that their betrayal of you was related to how you've been treating them.

Again, whatever shortcomings you may have shown don't *justify* what your partner did in betraying you. But your role in the relationship is part of the context—those circumstances we've referred to. Of course your partner should have talked to you about what was bothering them, rather than, say, having an affair (not to say that affairs are always about shortcomings in the primary relationship—often they're not). But they *didn't* talk to you, and they probably had understandable reasons why they didn't. Maybe they were afraid to bring up their concerns with you. Maybe that was because you weren't all that receptive when they tried.

If you want to rebuild trust, you'll need to tolerate the thought that your own attitudes and actions were part of the circumstances that led to the betrayal. That's a bitter pill to swallow. It doesn't mean you're to blame for your partner's bad behavior. But if you can't look at your own contribution to the state of your relationship, you won't be able to build trust.

Otherwise, you're stuck in a relationship in which one of you (your partner) is permanently the convicted villain, and the other (you) is permanently judge, jury, and jailer. Would you want that kind of relationship? Would you want to be with a partner who would accept that kind of relationship?

I suppose if that sounds good to you, there's not much point in trying to establish trust. But if that's what you wanted, I doubt you'd have read this far. That's more or less how Elsie felt (recall that her husband Charles was hiring prostitutes) when the couple first came to see me, and it wasn't working for either of them.

No, building trust isn't about either of you being the villain. It's about each of you coming to see what happened in all its shades of gray, recognizing that both of you were somehow part of what led to where you are. It's about forming a richer understanding of each other, so you can look back on the betrayal and its context and see how something like that can happen to two basically good people.

That last idea, that you're both basically good people, is really the essence of trust. If you can't find a way of reconciling what you each did with the idea that you're decent human beings, you can't rebuild trust.

Building trust is the antidote to that awful feeling you had when you first found out about the betrayal: "Who are you? I thought I knew you!" When you've built trust, you can say, "*Now* I see where you were coming from. I wish I had known this sooner, but at least I'm no longer mystified."

Of course, sometimes you realize as you develop that richer understanding of each other that the betrayal was just a symptom of a terminally ill relationship. A classic example is when a partner in a heterosexual marriage comes out as gay, often after years of refusing to acknowledge it to themselves. As painful as that realization can be for both partners, it also can bring about rebuilt trust. *Okay, now I understand why you did what you did. We need to split up, but I'm glad to be able to trust you again.*

But often, when partners are able to understand the circumstances that led to the betrayal, and each of their contributions to those circumstances, they can stay together with greater confidence than they had before. They're the couples who often express gratitude for the growth they've experienced both individually and as a couple. They're the couples who say they've come to realize that something had to happen, and, painful as it was, they're glad it did, because they're so much better off now.

Getting to the "Oh, Shit!" Moment

How do you get to this wonderful mutual understanding I've been touting as the key to building trust?

Even if you've been able to let go of your anger, you might still be struggling to make sense out of what your partner did. How do you square what they did with your sense of that person you thought you knew? How can you come to trust that person again?

And how can your partner square what you did with their sense of the person—you—that they thought they knew?

There's no magic formula for gaining mutual understanding of the betrayal. How do you develop any kind of understanding? It's a combination of experiences and how you think about those experiences. The more you're free of panic—in other words, the more you've actually forgiven what happened—the more you'll be able to talk about it, think about it, and reconsider your assumptions about it.

As I said, there's no magic formula. But one guideline to help you get to the kind of understanding I've been talking about is to look for the "Oh, shit!" moment.

What's the "Oh, shit!" moment?

Well, it's not the sudden, loud "Oh, shit!" you might say when you've hit your thumb with a hammer. It's the slow, quiet "Oh, shit!" you say when you realize why something is so difficult. It's short for "Oh, shit—*now* I see why this is so hard!"

The "Oh, shit!" moment is the dawning realization that there are good, non-crazy reasons why you are the way you are, and your partner is the way they are. And that means you have a glimmer of understanding why they did what they did—even though it was a betrayal. You still don't like it, and wish they hadn't done it. But you can start to see why they did it.

Of course, the "Oh, shit!" moment isn't just a moment. We rarely come to understand painful realities in a blinding flash of insight. It's usually based on a series of small realizations over time. But the sense of recognition that you've come to a new, richer understanding of what happened can be dramatic.

For Greta and Van, the "Oh, shit!" moment happened after four sessions of couples therapy. At the fifth session, Van described a conversation between him and Greta a few days before. Greta told him she was planning another trip to see her parents (recall that her father had molested her when she was a child, and her mother had refused to believe Greta when she told her about it). Ever since Greta had told him about the abuse after years of keeping it secret, Van's reaction to Greta's planning a trip to see her parents had been anger. But this time, something had shifted for him.

Instead of storming out or picking a fight, Van took a breath and said to Greta, "You know, I think I need to get a better sense of how you manage to be okay taking care of your parents. I'm guessing it must be hard for you. And I know my getting pissed about it hasn't helped. Can you help me understand what it's like for you?"

In our session, Greta said she didn't know how to react at first. She felt a mix of relief that Van wasn't mad, gratitude that he seemed to be trying to understand her, and anger when she thought about all the times he had been so hurtful. But after a few tearful moments she responded, "I know it's been hard for you too." They went on to talk about the whole situation in ways they never had before.

What made this possible? Neither Van nor Greta could pinpoint a particular moment in our work that made the difference, and I couldn't either. But I do know that Van could only have opened up to understanding Greta's experience when he felt validated himself. And what our sessions provided was a space where both of them could feel that sense of validation.

The "Oh, shit!" moment doesn't solve your problems. (That's why I don't call it the "Aha!" moment.) But it does mark a turning point. The "Oh, shit!" moment is when you stop insisting that reality be different from what it is. And that means you stop squabbling about it. *I wish you hadn't felt that way. But I can see why you did. And I can see why I felt the way I did. Now what?*

You can't force the "Oh, shit!" moment, but you can help it happen simply by knowing that it's possible. How can you know that it's possible? The key is to accept that what happened, painful as it was, had a valid basis for both of you.

In other words, the key is a mindset of faith.

Trust and Faith

Even to try to rebuild trust with a partner is itself an expression of faith. You don't know if it will work out or not. You don't know how you'll feel going forward, and you don't know how your partner will feel going forward.

But when you're able to look at the betrayal as a painful but understandable consequence of how things were—even though you didn't see it coming—then you're able to consider building trust. And that attitude is what I mean by faith.

I've noted before that the one option you *don't* have is to go back to how things were before the betrayal. Do you see why? To go back to how things were wouldn't be rebuilding trust; it would be denying reality. The way things were is what led to the betrayal. No, if you're going to rebuild trust it will have to be based on reality, not denial.

Back in Chapter 12 I talked about my seven-word formula, "Be kind, don't panic, and have faith." I added the last two words ("have faith") when I observed that the couples who did well handling difficult problems—such as betrayal—were the ones who were able to find meaning in what had happened, rather than try to deny or suppress it. That's what I mean by faith.

And, as I've mentioned, the couples who show that kind of faith often express gratitude for the growth they've experienced as a result of the crisis of betrayal. I've never heard anyone say, "Thanks for cheating!" But I've often heard someone say something like, "This has been hard, but I'm so glad we've gone through it."

Can You Stay Together Without Trust?

Whether or not you are able to rebuild trust, you'll still need to decide if you want to stay together as partners or not.

If you've been able to rebuild trust, and you both want to stay together, well—great! You're one of those couples I mentioned a couple of paragraphs ago.

But what if you've decided you can't rebuild trust that your partner won't betray you again?

In that case, you'll probably want to split up. I say probably, because some people decide to stay together even when they don't trust that their partner wouldn't betray them again.

In Chapter 13 I talked about people who don't feel they have the option of splitting up. They're going to stay in the relationship, trust or no.

But I've worked with other people who feel they *could* split up, but don't want to give up the life they've built with their partner even if they no longer trust them.

How can you stay with someone you don't trust without living in constant anxiety? Essentially, you need to change your expectations.

Remember Kimberly and Matt? After Matt confessed—only after getting busted—to his continued cheating, Kimberly couldn't find a way to trust his assurances that he wouldn't do it again. But, at least while we were working together, she still didn't want to split up. And she found a way to live with her decision with some degree of equanimity.

She told Matt that she couldn't believe his assurances, at least not yet. She realized that he might cheat again. She thought that if that happened she'd probably decide to split up, but she also recognized that she wouldn't know that for sure unless it happened.

After all, a year ago she would have said she'd never stay with a partner who had been unfaithful—and yet she had.

But she also felt that if it happened again, she wouldn't be devastated. She would strongly disapprove, but she wouldn't be caught by surprise. And that meant that her sense of well-being was no longer contingent on Matt's fidelity. She had changed her expectation—not her expectation that her husband wouldn't cheat, but her expectation that her essential well-being depended on his not cheating.

This way of coping gave Kimberly the emotional space she needed to figure out what she wanted, without being in constant fear. And it forced Matt to figure out what he wanted also. It also meant that their sense of intimacy, both sexually and more generally, was greatly reduced. Kimberly wasn't about to make herself vulnerable, and Matt soon realized that his attempts to connect with her just backfired.

I've known couples who continued in that mode for decades. As long as their fear of splitting up outweighs their pain from the lack of intimacy, they stay together.

So yes, you can stay together even if you can't rebuild trust. And you can find ways of living that let you tolerate it.

But, as I said, if you can't rebuild trust, you'll probably want to split up.

Splitting Up and Also Rebuilding Trust

We've been talking in this chapter about rebuilding trust with a spouse or committed partner when there's been a betrayal. In Chapter 15 we'll talk about rebuilding trust in other relationships.

But before we go there, let's consider what happens when you decide to end a committed partnership—in a marriage, this means divorce.

Some couples are able to make a complete break, meaning they have no intention of further contact after they've taken care of the logistics of splitting up. Usually those couples don't have children together (though Flora's situation, in which she was escaping a violent husband who was the father of her children, is all too common).

When it's one partner who is driving the breakup—as is almost always the case—then this can be difficult at first, especially for the other partner. It can be emotionally messy. But eventually, each former partner usually moves on. And for them, moving on doesn't have to mean rebuilt trust—after all, they're no longer in each other's lives.

But what about couples who need to remain in each other's lives? The quintessential example, of course, is a couple who have kids together, and will be co-parenting after they separate. And there are other situations that mean that a separated couple will still have an active relationship. I've worked with couples who divorce but stay in business together. I've worked with couples who divorce but continue to share a house.

If you're going to continue to be involved in each other's lives, you'll want to rebuild trust with each other. But the nature of the trust to be rebuilt will be different, because your expectations of each other will change when you split up.

As we talked about in Chapters 2 and 3, your sense of betrayal was determined by the expectations of the relationship you had with the person who betrayed you. And when you transform the relationship, you're transforming those expectations.

As an obvious example, your ex-spouse can have sex with other people without betraying you. If you're co-parenting with them, you'll still want to build a relationship of trust with them to help you handle parenting issues, but you don't have to worry about whom they're sleeping with, except in terms of how that might affect your kids. (Yes, I know you might still have an emotional reaction when you find out your ex-spouse has moved to someone else, even if you're the one who initiated the divorce. That's because we're all bundles of mixed feelings, and some parts of us take longer to accept new realities.)

Essentially, when you split up with a partner, you've changed to a non-couple relationship. How might you rebuild trust in non-couple relationships? That's the topic of Chapter 15.

Reflections on Chapter 14

1. Take stock of where you are on the journey of healing from betrayal. (If you're not dealing with betrayal, imagine that you are.) Do you feel you've mostly forgiven the betrayal, in the sense of letting go of the anger? If not, what would help you get there?
2. If you were betrayed by a partner, to what extent do you trust that they wouldn't betray you again? Depending on how long it's been since you discovered the betrayal, your trust level probably fluctuates a lot. What seems to affect your trust level?
3. How does the concept of the "Oh, shit!" moment strike you? Have you had moments in which you've been able to get a glimmer of understanding what happened?
4. When I talked in the chapter about your own part in creating the circumstances of your relationship, how did you feel? Can you recognize that you're partly responsible for how your relationship has developed, without taking blame or responsibility for the choices your partner made? This is often a tough one.
5. If you're deciding whether or not to stay in the relationship with a partner who betrayed you, how important will trust be to you? Can you imagine staying in the relationship without trusting your partner?
6. If you decide to split up, will you still have a relationship with your ex-partner? Can you imagine trust—a different kind of trust, based on different expectations—with your ex-partner?

Chapter 15

Rebuilding Trust in Other Relationships

How Important is the Relationship?

In Chapter 14 we talked about rebuilding trust in a couple relationship. What about other relationships?

Lori and Phyllis were both best friends and business partners. When Lori found out that Phyllis had failed to file taxes for their business for five years, exposing them to enormous potential liability, she felt betrayed. How could Phyllis have done that? And how could they move on with either their friendship or their business partnership?

Sally had been abandoned by her mother and neglected by her father. She got away from her father as soon as she could and cut off contact. Then her big brother Ed, who had always been protective, told her boyfriend she had been cheating, and she cut Ed off too.

This was all many years ago. She knew a lot had changed—in particular, she had heard her father had turned things around, though she hadn't felt ready to reach out to him. Now Ed was inviting her to help him care for their father, who was terminally ill. She wanted to heal the breaches with both her father and her brother. But how could she get past her experience of betrayal from both of them?

How do you move on when someone has betrayed you? Just as in the case of couple relationships, you'll need to decide whether you want to maintain the relationship—in other words, work to rebuild trust—or find some way to split up.

But with non-couple relationships, exactly what "splitting up" means is more complicated.

Of course, if the relationship isn't all that important to you, you can simply end it. If a contractor does a poor job and won't make it right, just don't use that contractor again.

What about relationships that *are* important to you? To lose a dear friend is often an occasion for deep grief. To lose a business partner can create painful difficulties not unlike the dislocations of divorce, involving financial loss and legal disputes. Lori was faced with both of these possibilities, and had to decide if either of her relationships with Phyllis, as best friend and as business partner, could be healed.

If you're in that sort of situation, it's not an easy choice, but you do have options. You can decide to maintain those relationships—and try to heal the hurt from the betrayal—or you can decide to terminate them. Being a friend or business partner is a consensual relationship that either party can terminate if they want to.

But when you've been betrayed by your mother or father or sibling or adult child, you don't have the same choices available. Because you can't actually "split up" with them.

You Can't "Split Up" with Your Mother

You might think you can. Indeed, you can cut off contact. But *you can't actually end a relationship that you don't have the power to define.* You can end a marriage by divorcing someone. But you can't change who your family is.

That's not just a technicality. Your parents or siblings or children stay your parents or siblings or children whether you're in touch or not, and that fact has ramifications, both emotional and social, that you don't control.

What ramifications? Don't you get to decide whether you let people be in your life or not?

Cutoffs Come At a Cost

Well, yes—you do get to decide if you want to cut someone out of your life or not.

But family relationships have ripples that extend beyond you. Your presence or absence at the family wedding or the Sunday dinner or the hospital bedside isn't just about you. Family estrangements can have multigenerational effects that leave grandchildren wondering where they came from, and cousins wondering why they can't talk to other cousins they've never met.

Karl Pillemer is a sociologist who has studied the effects of family estrangements. For his book *Fault Lines: Fractured Families and How to Mend Them*, Pillemer interviewed hundreds of people involved in family estrangement about how they've been affected. Based on his research he estimated that at least a quarter of Americans are currently estranged from a family member. If you're one of them, you're not alone.

Pillemer also found that over 80% of those people who were estranged were upset about the estrangement. He doesn't break that number down in terms of who initiated the estrangement, and it could be that most of those people who are upset were the ones who were dumped, not the ones doing the dumping. Nevertheless, he found that family estrangement is a very common occurrence, and it's associated with enormous suffering, whether you're the dumper or the dumpee.

In my work with people who are estranged from family members—and, consistent with Pillemer's research, I've met many—I've seen that suffering. The metaphor we often use for estrangement, "cutting off," is apt, because to the people involved it's like an amputation. It might be necessary to save the patient's life, but it leaves something missing. And the phantom limb can still hurt.

Sally realized this. Even though she was the one who initiated the cutoffs with both her father and her brother, she had always felt their absence keenly.

Regarding her father, Sally never regretted her decision to cut off contact. Getting away from him felt like saving her life at the time.

But regarding her brother Ed, Sally remembered how he had been her best friend, and how she had counted on him to have her back. When Ed told her boyfriend about her seeing other guys, Sally was so hurt and angry that she couldn't see any solution other than cutting Ed out of her life. But she missed his loving presence in her life.

Sally's willingness to work on healing both relationships was only possible because the circumstances had changed. Her father had become clean. Her own living situation was stable. And, with maturity, she was able to have some perspective on what her brother had done, and her own role in it. But she said she wished she had known how painful cutting her brother out of her life would be—if she had known, maybe she would have tried to find a way to get past his betrayal of her and rebuild trust, rather than cutting him off.

Cutting someone in your family out of your life is a choice you can make, but it's drastic. If you do a web search, you can find thousands of sites that urge you to do so, and tell you how to do it. But those sites rarely invite you to consider the downside.

How can you rebuild trust after a betrayal? We considered how that can happen for couples in Chapter 14. What about for other relationships?

Rebuilding Trust in Non-Couple Relationships

If you do want to rebuild trust with someone, the way forward is similar to what we talked about for couples in Chapter 14.

I'm assuming, of course, that you've been able to (mostly) forgive what they did—forgive in the sense we've talked about in this book, which means letting go of the anger. As I've pointed out, forgiving someone doesn't mean you trust them, or that you want to stay in contact with them. It just means you're not fighting with the reality of what happened anymore.

If you want to go further and rebuild trust with someone, you'll need to develop an understanding of what happened that lets you see both your own reactions and the other person's reactions as consistent with being a decent person. It's the "Oh, shit!" moment—that dawning realization that you can understand why they acted how they did, even as you understand why you acted as you did.

As I mentioned regarding couples, the "Oh, shit!" moment doesn't dictate how to proceed. You might conclude that what the person did *isn't* consistent with being a decent person, in which case there's no point trying to develop trust. But I think—and perhaps you do too—that most people are fundamentally decent. If someone does something hurtful, there's probably some non-evil basis for it that I can try to understand, even if what they did was morally wrong.

What Kind of Trust Do You Need?

In terms of building trust, the big difference between couple and non-couple relationships is about the *kind* of trust you need to build to stay in contact with someone.

To decide to stay married to someone, most of us want to be confident that they'll be transparent about their finances, their sexual relationships, and their family commitments. Moreover, we'd want to be confident that we can at least tolerate sharing space with them.

By contrast, being friends with someone doesn't entail nearly the same level of expectations. My friends don't owe me financial or sexual transparency, and I (usually) don't have to live with them. What I need to trust to keep in contact with a friend, then, is very different from what I need to trust to stay with a spouse.

What about family ties?

The trust expectations in family relationships are generally in between those for spouses and those for friends. In fact, many of the difficulties that lead to family members feeling betrayed are based on different assumptions about those expectations. Those differences can be especially acute when two people come together as partners, each bringing along their own family's ideas about what they owe their parents, siblings, and in-laws.

Greta continued to stay in contact with her aging parents, in spite of her father's having molested her and her mother's failure to believe her, because she felt an obligation to do so. Adult children, she felt, need to take care of their parents, even when their relationship has been difficult.

Was she crazy to do so? Did her efforts on their behalf reflect a complete lack of self-care? Van thought so, at first. But when they were both calm enough to talk about it, Greta was able to help Van understand that she wasn't a victim. She was able to keep herself safe, and didn't need to let those past experiences completely define her relationship with her parents. And she was better off doing so.

I've worked with parents who felt betrayed when their adult daughter didn't tell them about a new relationship for a month. I've also worked with adult children who felt betrayed when their parents sell their childhood home without consulting them. It's not for me to define what should or shouldn't constitute betrayal.

But rebuilding trust in those relationships is a lot easier when you're able to reconsider your expectations. You might not be able to trust that your kids or your parents will always keep you in the loop about everything in their lives. But maybe you can still stay in touch even if they don't.

Are You Sure You Need an Apology?

You're trying to rebuild trust with someone—let's say a family member—who has betrayed you. And you want to trust that they understand the hurt they caused, genuinely regret it, and have resolved not to do it again.

Doesn't that call for an apology?

We'll talk more about apologies in Chapter 16, which is all about how you can recover from betrayal if you're the one who did the betraying. As we'll see, an apology can be very helpful as a step toward repairing a breach.

But if you're the one who was betrayed, *requiring* an apology from the person who betrayed you is often a trap. Yes, you want the person to acknowledge the hurt they caused, and you fear that if they don't acknowledge what they did they might do it again. Not a crazy thing to want.

But the problem is that the person who betrayed you might be feeling you betrayed them too, and they might be waiting for you to apologize to them. Or even if they're not waiting for an apology, your insistence on an apology might leave them fearing that you just want to punish them, not reconnect with them.

And, if you search your soul, that fear might be at least partly accurate.

A few pages ago I mentioned Karl Pillemer's book about family estrangements. Among the hundreds of people he interviewed, he found a subset who had attempted reconciliation with the family member from whom they were estranged. Every single person he talked to who had attempted reconciliation was glad they had done so. Not all of their efforts to reconcile were successful, but even the people whose efforts failed were glad they had tried.

When reconciliation efforts succeeded, one of the keys Pillemer identified was that the person reaching out to reconcile gave up on the need for an apology as a precondition. They would reconnect without trying to rehash what happened, often recognizing that ending the cutoff was more important than needing to be understood.

Of course, you'll only try reconnecting without an apology if two things are true. First, you need to be past the anger—in other words, you've forgiven what had happened. Second, you need to feel safe enough to see what would happen if you try to reconnect. Flora would never try to reconnect with her unrepentant, violent ex-husband, even though she wasn't angry anymore. But you might be able to try reconnecting with that brother who insulted your fiancé fifteen years ago. Or with your mother who criticized your parenting last month.

Curiously, Pillemer's respondents found that once they had re-established contact, an apology often came later. If you can get past the need for agreement on what happened, you might find that your positions soften, and you can each start to see the nuances rather than being stuck in black-and-white. That's when your relative might well express remorse for what they did—and you might feel moved to do the same.

As I mentioned earlier in this chapter, the kind of trust you need to establish to stay with a committed partner is generally different from the kind of trust you need to establish to stay in contact in another relationship. You might not want to stay with a partner if you can't come to a mutual understanding of what happened.

But in other relationships, you don't always need the same level of trust. If you can relax your expectations, you might find that continuing or re-establishing contact is preferable to a cutoff, even if it means the relationship feels superficial for a time. Letting go of what you thought you needed, paradoxically, can be the key to getting it after all.

Reflections on Chapter 15

1. Are you currently estranged from a family member? If so, how has the estrangement affected you? You probably have mixed feelings—how would you describe the mix?
2. If you're estranged from a family member, what sort of trust would you need to rebuild to be able to re-establish contact? What sort of trust could you do without? For example, might you be able to let go of the need for them to understand your experience, and settle for being able to be cordial when you get together at family events?
3. Are you holding out for an apology? Could you consider letting go of that need?

Chapter 16

What If You're the Betrayer?

We've All Hurt Loved Ones

Up to now we've focused on how to heal if you've been betrayed. We've talked about reconsidering your expectations, how to get to forgiveness, and whether and how to rebuild trust with someone who betrayed you, as you move on.

But what if you're the one who betrayed someone else? How can you hope to heal the relationship? How can you gain forgiveness?

Of course, you might be reading this chapter because a loved one feels you betrayed them, and they want you to read this as part of the healing process. If that's you, welcome.

Or you might be reading this chapter because you feel terrible about what you did, and are hoping to find ways of repairing the damage in your relationship. Welcome to you too.

But I think this chapter is for all of us, whether we've been betrayed or been the betrayer—because we've all betrayed someone at one time or another.

I know that's an exaggeration. As I mentioned in Chapter 2, the term "betrayal" implies failing someone in an important way, not merely annoying someone. We haven't all cheated on our spouses, or abused loved ones, or run up massive debts and lied about them.

But if you're involved with someone long enough, you're likely to have hurt them in a significant way. That's the human condition— we all screw up on occasion. And some of those hurts might have risen to the level of betrayal, at least in the eyes of someone who never expected you'd hurt them that way.

In other words, we're all in this together. However you enter this chapter, whether you see yourself as an injured betrayed or a guilty betrayer, I hope you'll recognize that we're all both sometimes, at least to some extent. As I noted when we talked about forgiveness, we're all doing the best we can under the circumstances. That's a message of faith—which is the key to healing.

What If You Don't Think You Did Anything Wrong?

You're hoping to heal your relationship with someone who feels you betrayed them. What if you don't think you did anything wrong?

Well, betrayal isn't always about right and wrong. As we've discussed, betrayal is about failing to meet what someone expects of you based on their relationship with you.

Remember Teresa and James? After four years together, Teresa told James she realized she didn't want children. From the start of their relationship, Teresa had said she's open to the idea of having children, just not ready yet. James felt betrayed.

Teresa felt bad for hurting James. But did she do anything morally wrong? She felt she had been responding honestly to James whenever the subject of having children came up. When she finally had some clarity, she told him what she had decided. She could even understand why James felt betrayed. But healing from this wouldn't involve her confessing to wrongdoing—because she didn't feel she had done anything wrong.

It's certainly possible that your situation is similar. Maybe you feel you didn't do anything wrong, like Teresa. Maybe your partner's expectations of you were unrealistic—Patricia's thinking that Zach's masturbation was tantamount to infidelity, for example. Maybe someone had expectations of you that you disagree with morally, such as Sally's expectation that her brother Ed would put loyalty to her above transparency with the boyfriend she was cheating on.

All possible. Which is to say, maybe this is all the other person's problem, not yours.

But that's a bad assumption if you're looking to heal the relationship. You're better off starting with the assumption that you *did* do something wrong—if not morally wrong, at least relationally inept. That's how the other person is viewing what you did, and if you hope that they'll want to stay in a relationship with you, you'll need to understand why they feel that way. Yes, you probably had your reasons for doing what you did, but your actions had painful consequences. You'll need to face up to that.

Even if you've given up on the relationship, and just want to accept that it's over and move on, you'll benefit by examining what you did, with specific attention to how your actions would lead someone to feel betrayed.

It's a painful journey, but I promise you it's worth the pain.

You Need to Forgive Too

Whatever level of guilt you may or may not feel, if you're hoping to heal the relationship with someone who feels you betrayed them, you're hoping they'll forgive you. You want their forgiveness, and maybe forgiveness from others—extended family, friend networks, the community at large. You can't force that to happen, but later in this chapter we'll talk about how you can make it easier for them.

But you don't just need forgiveness from others. You need to forgive too.

You've been hurt by what happened. Even if it's a clear-cut case of wrongdoing on your part, you've still been hurt by how others have treated you about it. As I noted in Chapter 14, maybe you deserved their anger—but if you're going to rebuild a relationship, you'll need to be able to trust them again. And that means you'll need to let go of your own anger about how you were treated. In other words, you'll need to find a way to forgive.

Of course, some of your anger toward the person you betrayed might predate your betrayal, and perhaps contributed directly to your deciding to do what you did. Many people who cheat on their partners describe a progression of building resentments that culminated in their feeling justified in cheating. If you're hoping to rebuild a relationship, you'll need to find a way past those resentments, so you can work on the problems that led to them.

How can you do that? Well, eight chapters in this book (Chapters 4 through 11) are all about how to forgive. The three steps to forgiveness apply to you too: forgive yourself, forgive those who hurt you, and forgive God.

Three Steps to Forgiveness When You're the Betrayer

First, you'll need to forgive yourself.

In Chapter 9 I explained why this is necessary even for people who have been hurt through no fault of their own. Of course, when you've betrayed someone you *were* the cause. Whether you feel what you did was morally wrong or not, you caused enormous pain to someone you care about.

It won't surprise you when I observe that forgiving yourself is often difficult when you've betrayed someone.

In the days after Kimberly found out that Matt had been cheating on her for much of the time they were doing couples therapy, she was livid. Matt, for his part, alternated between abject submission and angry defiance. Part of the time he pleaded for Kimberly's forgiveness, and part of the time he reiterated that he had said he was sorry and won't do it again, so she should get past it.

Neither of those responses was helpful for Kimberly, or for Matt himself. Both his pleading and his dismissiveness were defensive reactions. For Matt to be able to act accountably, he would need to reflect on the consequences of his actions, and feel appropriately guilty, without dissolving into shame or panic. His defensive reactions were all about deflecting that shame or panic. Until he could think about what he did and why, his protestations that he was sorry and wouldn't do it again would ring hollow. How could he know, if he couldn't explain to himself why he had done what he had done?

By contrast, consider Beth and Albert. Beth had told Albert she wanted to separate after 40 years of marriage to pursue a relationship with a man she had met through her work. This had blindsided Albert, and they sought out couples work initially to help them figure out how to proceed with the separation. After Beth moved out, the man she was seeing dumped her, in part because he could sense that

Beth was still emotionally attached to Albert. Beth realized that she still wanted to work on the marriage, and Albert agreed.

In our first session after they agreed to work on the marriage, Beth reiterated her deep regret for the pain she caused Albert. She knew it was wrong of her to have pursued another relationship—which, she acknowledged, actually had involved sexual infidelity while she was still with Albert—rather than confront the problems she was having in the marriage.

But she realized that those problems in the marriage were real. Rather than plead for Albert to accept her back, she asked him to work with her on those issues. Neither Albert nor Beth was certain they would be able to make it work, but they also realized that they wanted to try.

Beth had recognized that her having the affair was wrong. She regretted it. But she also realized that under the circumstances—including what she did and didn't know about herself—her behavior reflected who she was at the time, and she could accept that she was doing the best she could.

In other words, Beth was able to forgive herself.

It's a marvelous irony that you'll have to grant yourself some compassionate understanding in order to fully accept responsibility for the bad stuff you did. If you're overwhelmed by self-loathing, you won't be able to think about what you did, much less hear from others about how it affected them.

For the other two steps, forgiving those who hurt you and forgiving God, I'll refer you back to Chapters 10 and 11. When you can accept that we're *all* doing the best we can under the circumstances (forgiving others), and that this whole reality business is basically right to be what it is (forgiving God), you can get on with the hard work of figuring out how to move forward.

In particular, once you've been through the three steps to forgiveness, you'll be ready to try to clean up the mess. And the converse is also true: if you haven't forgiven, your attempts to clean up the mess won't work. Beth's efforts to reconnect with Albert offered him a chance to feel validated. Matt's efforts to reconnect with Kimberly just reinforced her sense that he was clueless about how he had hurt her.

Making Amends

The phrase "making amends" will be familiar to those of you in 12-step programs such as Alcoholics Anonymous, and I'm using it in the same way. Step 8 says to make a list of the people you've hurt, and Step 9 says to make direct amends to them, "except when to do so would injure them or others."

You don't have to be in a 12-step program to appreciate the idea. If you've betrayed someone, you've hurt them. Making amends is about trying to help them heal in whatever way you can. Of course, this not only benefits the person you've hurt; it also benefits you. To the extent that you feel guilty—appropriately—about what you did, helping the person you hurt feel better will help you feel better too.

And, of course, you need to take care that your efforts to relieve yourself of your guilt don't cause further harm. That's the cautionary part of Step 9.

How can you make amends when you've betrayed someone? And how can you avoid causing further harm?

Some actions are simple to define, albeit painful to carry out. If what you did cost someone money, pay it back. If you lied about someone to others, tell them you lied and set the record straight. If you damaged property, pay what it cost to repair the damage.

But how can you make amends when you've been sexually unfaithful? Or when you've caused someone to fear for their safety? Or when you've failed to fulfill important obligations to them in the past? When what you've done can't be undone, how do you repair the damage?

Sometimes you can't. If the person you betrayed has decided to cut off contact with you, the best you can do is to avoid further harm and respect their boundary. Learn from the experience, resolve to do better, and move on.

But if the person you betrayed is open to continuing a relationship with you, you might want to apologize.

Apologies, Non-Apologies, and Bullshit

Before we get into why and how to apologize, let's consider what clearly doesn't help.

As those of you who've studied philosophy might know, the word "apology" didn't originally imply that anyone was sorry. On the contrary, until around the time of Shakespeare the word meant a verbal defense rather than an expression of regret. Far from being sorry, the speaker of an apology was seeking to justify something. Plato's *Apology* is a defense of Socrates, not an acknowledgement of anything he did wrong. The word is still used in that way sometimes—for example, an "apologetics Bible" is designed to help its readers defend their faith.

I mention that bit of etymology because we've all heard apologies—I mean in the modern sense, supposedly conveying regret—that are actually more like justifications, minimizations, or excuses. Here are two of my favorites:

- If you were offended by what I did, I'm very sorry. That wasn't my intention.
- I don't know why I did it—it's just not me to do something like that. That's not who I am.

The first example, with the "if" clause, is essentially telling the person you hurt that you're sorry if they are so oversensitive that they would be offended by something that any sane person could see was innocent. And they're not only oversensitive—they're also unfair. After all, shouldn't they judge you by your intentions?

Strangely, the person you say that to won't be filled with gratitude for your assessment that they're crazy. And if, say, I just stomped on someone's toe, my protest that I didn't *intend* to stomp on their toe rather misses the point.

That first example qualifies as a classic non-apology apology.

The second example is more complex. You're acknowledging that you did something bad, but then asking the person you hurt not to hold you responsible for doing it. After all, that just wasn't you to do something like that.

Who else did it, then? If you're pleading insanity, in the sense that you were having a psychotic break, or perhaps were under the control of a dissociated personality, that might elicit some compassion, but won't, and shouldn't, elicit trust. If you were nuts and have no idea why you did what you did, how could someone trust that you won't do it again?

And if you're not pleading insanity, the technical term for claiming "that's not who I am" is "bullshit." It *is* who you are, or at least it was who you were when you did what you did. Your worst actions don't define *all* of who you are. But if you're not able to accept that you're the one who did what you did, your "apology" will be nonsense.

Do you see the connection between forgiving yourself and being able to own what you did? When you've stopped being angry at yourself for what you did, you don't have to duck accountability for it. You can even understand why the person you hurt would be angry at you, and not be horrified by their reactions.

Which means you have to be well along in forgiving yourself before you attempt an apology, if you have any hope that the apology will help heal your relationship with the person you betrayed.

Why Apologize?

If you've forgiven yourself sufficiently that you can own what you did, you might be ready to offer an apology. But before you do so, you need to consider what you hope to accomplish. Why should you apologize, anyway? What are you hoping will happen when you apologize?

You might be hoping to reconcile, to rebuild trust with the person you betrayed so that they'll be willing to heal your relationship with them. Not a bad thing to want.

But there's a Catch-22. If you're apologizing because you're desperate to get the person you betrayed to reconcile, it probably won't work. They won't trust your reassurances. Remember Matt and Kimberly? Matt's telling Kimberly how sorry he was for cheating on her was mostly about trying to get her to reassure him that he could stay, and she could see that. It was more about asking her to relieve his pain than about helping relieve her pain.

No, offering an apology in hopes of convincing someone to change their mind won't work. But an apology *can* help you both heal—if your focus is on recognizing the effects of what you did on the person you hurt, rather than on yourself.

There's no guarantee that the person you betrayed will reconcile with you after you apologize. But, ironically, your letting go of the need for that guarantee makes your apology more credible, which might help the person you betrayed trust you again.

One more caveat about apologizing. For your apology to be credible, you have to believe it yourself. If you believe you didn't do anything that warrants an apology, don't attempt to apologize. Your insincerity will be obvious.

As I mentioned earlier in this chapter, if someone feels you betrayed them, there's probably something in your own behavior you should look at carefully. And that might lead you to want to offer an apology that you actually mean.

How Should You Apologize?

Let's look at some scenarios that might help you apologize effectively.

Lori and Phyllis were best friends and business partners for many years. They came to see me after Phyllis told Lori that she hadn't filed taxes for their company, and that the IRS might hold them personally responsible for thousands of dollars of unpaid taxes. Phyllis accepted that this situation was her own fault; she was the partner who handled the financial side of the business.

If you were Phyllis, how might you apologize to Lori? Here are some variations I've heard from people in similar situations:

- Looking back, I didn't handle this the way I should have. I'll straighten this out—don't worry about it. You don't have to make a big deal out of this.

- At first I just kept putting it off. Then I was afraid to tell you about it, because let's face it, you're not always easy to talk to. Anyway, we're here now—how do you want me to handle it?

- Please forgive me. I can't bear the thought of losing our friendship or our business together. Tell me what I can do to make up for this!

- I fucked up, big time. I didn't take care of it, and then the longer it went the more I was afraid to fix it. I can only imagine what this is putting you through, and how hard it must be for you to trust anything I'm saying. If you want to tell me about how this has affected you, I want to hear it.

Each of those variations is a sincere expression of how the person who said it was feeling. And, as I'm guessing you already realize, only the last one is potentially helpful for healing a relationship. Minimizing (as in the first example), deflecting blame (second example), and pleading (third example) don't help.

What about that fourth example makes it potentially helpful? In addition to clearly owning their responsibility for what they did, the person is focusing on the experience of the person they're apologizing to. The apology is about the person who got hurt, not about the person who hurt them.

And in that fourth example, the person doing the apologizing is recognizing that they might *not* fully understand the other person's experience. They're offering the other person a chance to tell them about it. You might think you know how you hurt them—but you might be wrong. In fact, you *can't* fully know someone else's experience. Acknowledging that invites the other person to risk being honest with you, because they sense you're open to hearing them.

What about apologizing when you've been sexually unfaithful? Here are some variations I've heard:

- I don't know how it happened—I was drunk. You know it didn't mean anything. Can't we just get back to how things were?
- Okay, I shouldn't have done it. If you weren't so cold, maybe I wouldn't be looking for it from someone else.
- I hate myself. Please don't leave me—I don't know how I could stand it.
- I'm so sorry. I'm trying to figure out why I would have cheated on you, when I know it's wrong. I can't expect you to trust me until I can trust myself, and I'm not there yet. If you want to tell me about how this has affected you, I want to listen.

Again, the first three examples won't get you anywhere. And again, the fourth example, with its focus on being open to the other person's experience, might invite them to risk reconnecting.

I've only rarely heard someone say something like that second sentence in the fourth example: *I can't expect you to trust me until I can trust myself, and I'm not there yet.* When I have heard it, it's been powerful, because it's credible. Sometimes, if the couple has separated, the person will follow that up by saying, "I don't think I should come back yet." If you say that, you're showing respect for both your partner and yourself. You don't want to come back only to have things go wrong again, and you're taking responsibility for that decision rather than blaming your partner for it.

You can only get to that level of credibility in your apology if you've deeply forgiven yourself. This is another instance of the irony I mentioned earlier in this chapter: you need to accept your own essential validity in order to tolerate the pain of accountability.

And when you can tolerate the pain of accountability, your apology might actually mean something to the person you betrayed. Perhaps the two of you will be able to work toward reconciliation.

What If They Won't Accept Your Apology?

You sincerely want to apologize for what you did. Maybe you hope to rebuild trust and continue the relationship, but even if that's not likely, you still want to offer an apology in hopes that it will help both of you move on.

As we've already noted, if the person you betrayed wants no contact with you, you'll just have to move on without having the chance to apologize to them. Learn what you need to learn and move on with life.

But what if you're able to offer an apology, but the person you betrayed won't accept it?

For example, you offer your apology, and the person says, "I hear that you're apologizing, but I don't believe you. You're just trying to get out of trouble with me." Or they might say, "I'm not ready to accept your apology." Or they might say, "I appreciate your offer, but I don't forgive you."

Of course you'd *want* the person you hurt to accept your apology. But offering an apology isn't about what you want. It's about trying to repair what you broke.

Ironically, your apology has a better chance of being accepted if you offer it without needing acceptance. When the person you hurt senses that what you're offering really is intended for their benefit—in other words, when they sense that you're not trying to manipulate them for your benefit—they might be able to accept what you're offering.

As you know, you can't determine when or if the person you betrayed will accept your apology. And even if they do accept your apology, you can't determine whether they will want to reconcile with you or not.

But just as you can't determine their reaction, they can't determine yours either. You can heal from this even if they aren't willing or able to help you.

Ultimately, offering a sincere apology benefits you whether the other person accepts it or not. In fact, being *able* to offer a sincere apology benefits you, whether or not you have the chance even to express it to the other person.

To face what you've done, forgive, and offer accountability are manifestations of faith. Faith is what will heal the person you betrayed, and faith is what will heal you too.

Reflections on Chapter 16

1. How did you find your way to this chapter? Are you someone who was betrayed, and you kept reading after Chapter 15 to get a sense of what I might say to betrayers? Are you a betrayer yourself, and were asked to read this chapter by someone you

betrayed? Are you both betrayed and betrayer? Or did you read it for some other reason (you're a therapist, or someone I've asked to read the book)?

2. If you've betrayed someone, do you feel that you did anything morally wrong, against your own values? If yes, to what extent have you been able to forgive yourself?

3. If you don't feel you did anything morally wrong, but still caused someone to feel betrayed, are there ways that in hindsight you might have handled the situation better? Can you forgive yourself for that?

4. If you've betrayed someone, have you offered an apology? If so, how did it go?

5. When I note that offering accountability is a manifestation of faith, how do you understand that? You might want to read (or re-read) Chapter 12. How does the idea of accepting your own essential validity as a person enable you to face what you did and offer a sincere apology?

Chapter 17

What Happened to Those Couples?

How Did It Turn Out?

We've met a dozen different couples, mostly married couples but some other relationships as well, in the course of this book. How did things turn out for them?

All of my example couples represent situations I've actually encountered. But, as I mentioned in Chapter 1, their identifying details have been thoroughly disguised. In some cases, this meant creating composite characters so as to avoid representing people in ways that could theoretically identify them. As you read what happened to each couple, consider the stories realistic, but not real.

I'll remind you of each couple's backstory here, but you might want to revisit Chapter 1 for a fuller picture.

Angie and Peter

Angie and Peter came to see me after Angie had told Peter she was no longer okay with his failing to produce significant income with his freelance writing, after three years of her working two jobs to make ends meet. He had agreed to come to therapy only when Angie gave him an ultimatum: therapy or divorce.

We had three sessions, during which Angie and Peter seemed to get to a better understanding of each other's concerns. They both reported that their sense of betrayal had lessened.

Then in their fourth session, Angie said that she had confronted Peter with evidence that he had been having an affair. At first he had denied it, but then admitted he had been having sex with an old girlfriend from high school he had reconnected with at a reunion. They agreed to separate.

Beth and Albert

Beth had told Albert that she wanted to separate after 40 years of marriage, because she had become emotionally involved with a man she met through work. When they first came to see me, they were working on how to separate. A couple of months later, after the relationship with the other man didn't pan out, Beth told Albert she wanted to work on their marriage, and they came back to couples therapy. Beth confessed to Albert that her relationship with the other man had indeed been sexual before she and Albert separated, as Albert had suspected.

In our sessions, both of them recognized that there had been long-standing issues in their marriage that they had avoided addressing. While Beth was deeply regretful about her infidelity, and they were both clear that the issues in the marriage didn't justify it, Albert was able to understand how it could have happened and forgive Beth. After about 20 sessions over the course of a year, they were expressing gratitude that the crisis had occurred, because they were both feeling much better off.

Elsie and Charles

When Elsie contracted herpes and found out that Charles had been hiring "escorts" on his frequent business trips for years, she was bitter and resentful. She agreed to come to couples therapy because she didn't want to give up their affluent lifestyle, and wanted to find a way to stay together. But she was clear she had no interest in forgiving Charles, much less recovering any sort of intimacy with him.

Charles just wanted to find a way of doing penance that Elsie could accept. He expressed the hope that they could go back to some kind of normalcy.

We had about 20 sessions over eight months, and they decided they didn't need to make more appointments. Elsie's assessment was that the therapy might have taken the edge off a little, but didn't make much difference. Charles said he had found some relief in being able to talk to Elsie with a referee present, and felt they could talk on their own now.

About five years after our last session, Charles wrote to tell me that Elsie had died after a year-long struggle with cancer. Charles took care of her to the end. Charles said that Elsie never expressed forgiveness, but did say she was grateful for his care.

Flora and Jason

Flora has been my exemplar of how you can forgive someone you don't trust. When I was working with her, her ex-husband Jason was still in prison.

We finished our work when Flora moved out of the area. As our sessions were winding down, Flora was notified that her ex would be eligible for parole, and she made contingency plans in case he tried to find her.

Frannie and Caleb

Frannie and Caleb came to couples therapy a few weeks after Frannie's father died suddenly, and Frannie found that she had been disinherited in her father's will. The only explanation Frannie could think of was that her father and Caleb had never got along well.

The crisis of this event brought out some tensions in their marriage. Frannie felt she couldn't talk with Caleb about her combined grief and sense of betrayal, partly because she felt Caleb bore some responsibility for what her father did. Caleb wanted to support Frannie, but his relationship with her father was always a sore point between them.

We worked together for about a year and a half. At first the focus was on what happened and how they could talk about it, but as they were more able to hear each other the work turned to other issues in their marriage, including a lack of intimacy that had developed over the years. Frannie still felt hurt by what her father had done, but both she and Caleb were grateful that the crisis had pushed them to work on their marriage.

Greta and Van

I've already described a lot of the work I did with Greta and Van. They first came to see me when Greta had told Van about having been sexually abused as a child by her father, and disbelieved by her mother when she told her about it. She had held this secret for decades even as she continued to maintain contact with her parents. Van was furious at Greta's parents, hurt by her keeping the secret from him, and incredulous that she would continue to visit and care for them.

As I described in earlier chapters, Greta and Van were not only able to forgive each other, they were also able to rebuild trust. I worked with them for about ten sessions over three months initially; in the years since then they've occasionally come back for what they refer to as a "tune-up" of a session or two. Greta's parents each died over the time I've known them. Their "tune-up" sessions have mostly focused on deepening their intimacy.

Kimberly and Matt

I've also told quite a bit of Kimberly and Matt's story in earlier chapters. We first met when Matt had moved out, had a brief sexual relationship with another woman, and moved back with Kimberly, which she allowed on condition that they do couples therapy. They did seven sessions and reported considerable improvement. Then Kimberly found out that Matt had been having an affair with a customer of his company. The customer told Kimberly what had been going on when Matt broke off the affair. She also told Matt's boss, which got him fired.

We met a few more times. At our last session, they said they had decided to divorce. Kimberly said she had made the decision, but Matt also expressed some relief.

Lori and Phyllis

Lori and Phyllis, friends and business partners, consulted me after Phyllis told Lori that they were in tax trouble, because she hadn't filed returns for their business for five years. Lori had trusted Phyllis to run the financial side of their business. Now she was wondering whether she could trust Phyllis even as a friend. She hoped seeing a couples therapist would help them decide how to move forward.

At our first session, Phyllis acknowledged that she had dropped the ball, but hoped that Lori would accept her apology and they could go on as before. Lori found that response completely inadequate. She could forgive what Phyllis had done, she said, but didn't know how to trust her.

We had four sessions, during which it didn't seem to me that much changed. I can't always tell if the work is helping or not, and either way I make a point of asking the people I'm working with what they think. In the first three sessions, both Lori and Phyllis said it had been helpful just to have someone to moderate their conversation. But at the fourth session, we left open future visits. I don't know if they stayed in business together, or stayed friends, or not.

Patricia and Zach

Patricia and Zach came to couples therapy with the understanding that Zach needed to address his sex addiction, which is how they characterized his masturbating to porn two or three times a week. Patricia considered both his masturbation and his porn use to be cheating. The only sex either one of them was supposed to have was with each other.

I described some of our work in Chapters 2 and 3. When Patricia thought about what really bothered her, she realized that it wasn't Zach's masturbating per se, but his focus on images of other women. As they were more able to talk about what was happening, they dropped the idea that Zach was a sex addict, and focused on their relationship with each other.

After meeting two or three times a month for four months, they decided to schedule a check-in session for six months later. At that session, they reported that their sex life in particular and their intimate life in general was much improved.

Sally and Ed

Sally and Ed, brother and sister, came to see me in hopes they could heal their estranged relationship. Sally had cut Ed out of her life 18 years before, after Ed had told Sally's then-boyfriend that she was cheating on him. She had already stopped contact with their father, who had been abusive, a few years before. Over the years, Sally had heard that their father had turned his life around, but she hadn't contacted him.

Recently, their father had become terminally ill. Ed, who had stayed in touch with their father and was involved in his care, contacted Sally to let her know. She realized how much she had missed having Ed in her life, and wanted to reconnect with their father as well.

When we met, it became clear to all of us that Sally and Ed had already accomplished most of what they needed to do to heal the relationship and move forward. Sally was able to forgive both her father and Ed, which also involved forgiving herself. And Ed was able to put what Sally did in perspective as well.

We met for a total of three sessions. What our sessions helped them do, they told me, was revisit their history with a safety net—in other words, my presence helped them feel confident that they could handle talking about the past without losing their cool.

Sarah and Phil

Sarah had discovered Phil, her husband of 30 years, dressed in women's clothing. After initially insisting that this was just a one-time occurrence, Phil later admitted that he had been concealing his cross-dressing from Sarah for their entire marriage. Sarah didn't know how to understand what Phil was doing. In spite of his assurances that he was not gay, and that he still loved and desired her and wanted to stay married, Sarah didn't know if she could believe him.

They met with me for twelve sessions over six months. At our last session Phil said he felt that Sarah understood him better, and Sarah agreed that she felt that way too. They were kinder to each other. But they also said their sex life, which had never been great, had disappeared entirely. Sarah didn't see a prospect of resuming sex with Phil—she said she was fine without it, and in any case couldn't imagine being with him after she saw him in women's clothing. Phil said he missed sexual intimacy with Sarah but could live without it. Neither of them wanted to break up. As I mentioned in Chapter 13, Sarah didn't see breaking up as a viable option.

Teresa and James

Teresa and James, both 30 years old and living together for four years, came to see me after Teresa told James she was clear that she didn't want to have children. Previously she had said she's open to having children, which James said was important to him. They still loved each other and didn't want to split up. But they both worried that this might be a deal-breaker.

I've worked with quite a few couples dealing with this issue, and most of the time it does turn out to be a deal-breaker. But over the course of six sessions, Teresa and James were able to resolve their dilemma and stay together.

As they explored how they each felt about having children, both Teresa and James found their attitudes shifting. Teresa realized that her misgivings about having a child reflected a view of herself as "bad seed." She loved being with babies and young children—she just felt that she couldn't be trusted to be a mother herself. The more she reflected on where this fear came from, the more she could separate from it.

The week before our fifth session, Teresa told James she had changed her mind—she now wanted to have a child with him. This left James worried that Teresa was caving in to pressure, and would come to resent her decision. They processed this in the fifth and sixth sessions.

When they decided to leave open future sessions, Teresa pointed out that their sense of resolution wasn't so much because they now had no doubts. Rather, they found that they could manage their doubts—they didn't need certainty.

I found that observation very moving, as a quintessential expression of faith. And I offer it as a blessing to you as you continue to heal from betrayal. May you find peace, joy, and strength in accepting the beautiful uncertainty of life.

Acknowledgements

Most of what I've learned about couples therapy, betrayal, and forgiveness comes from the thousands of people who have consulted me for help over the past thirty years. Thanks to all of them, and especially to those whose stories are reflected in the examples in this book.

I also thank the many colleagues and friends who helped shape and refine the ideas I've expressed. Special thanks to Gayle Belin, Michael Brown, Seth Chalmer, Jane Kast, Jean Pieniadz, and Sebastian Ryder for their detailed comments on earlier drafts of the book. Inclusion in that list doesn't imply agreement with everything I said, and remaining errors are my responsibility.

My wife and podcast co-host Judy Alexander is my first reader, incisive but kind bullshit detector, and heart's delight. She's also the author of beautiful erotic fiction. What I know about finding joy after experiencing loss, I know because of her.

About the Author

Dr. Bruce Chalmer is a psychologist in Vermont who has been working with couples for over thirty years. Through his teaching, consulting, writing, podcast, and videos about relationships, his ideas have helped thousands of couples and their therapists.

He has served in leadership positions in several Vermont Jewish communities, and is also a musician, composer, and choral director. He lives with his wife Judy Alexander in South Burlington. They have five adult children and six grandchildren.

For more information visit his website: https://brucechalmer.com

Together with Judy Alexander, he is the host of the *Couples Therapy in Seven Words* podcast, available anywhere you get your podcasts, or at https://ctin7.com.

References

Bos, Katrina (2017). *Tantric Intimacy: Discover the Magic of True Connection.* Tellwell Talent.

Fisher, H.E. (2011). Serial monogamy and clandestine adultery: Evolution and consequences of the dual human reproductive strategy. IN. S.C. Roberts (Ed.) *Applied Evolutionary Psychology.* Oxford University press.

Frankl, Viktor (1959). *Man's Search for Meaning.* Beacon Press.

Kort, Joe (2019). *Erotic Orientation.* Smart Sex – Smart Love Books.

Lamott, Anne (2000). Traveling Mercies: Some Thoughts on Faith. Anchor.

Pillemer, Karl (2020). *Fault Lines: Fractured Families and How to Mend Them.* Avery.

www.ingramcontent.com/pod-product-compliance
Lightning Source LLC
Chambersburg PA
CBHW060520130626
46553CB00002B/577